TEEN RIGHTS AND FREEDOMS

I Birth Control

TEEN RIGHTS AND FREEDOMS

| Birth Control

Noël Merino
Book Editor

GREENHAVEN PRESS
A part of Gale, Cengage Learning

GALE
CENGAGE Learning

Detroit • New York • San Francisco • New Haven, Conn • Waterville, Maine • London

Elizabeth Des Chenes, *Director, Content Strategy*
Cynthia Sanner, *Publisher*
Douglas Dentino, *Manager, New Product*

© 2014 Greenhaven Press, a part of Gale, Cengage Learning

WCN: 01-100-101

Gale and Greenhaven Press are registered trademarks used herein under license.

For more information, contact:
Greenhaven Press
27500 Drake Rd.
Farmington Hills, MI 48331-3535
Or you can visit our Internet site at gale.cengage.com.

For product information and technology assistance, contact us at:

Gale Customer Support, 1-800-877-4253.
For permission to use material from this text or product, submit all requests online at www.cengage.com/permissions.

Further permissions questions can be emailed to permissionrequest@cengage.com.

Articles in Greenhaven Press anthologies are often edited for length to meet page requirements. In addition, original titles of these works are changed to clearly present the main thesis and to explicitly indicate the author's opinion. Every effort is made to ensure the Greenhaven Press accurately reflects the original intent of the authors. Every effort has been made to trace the owners of copyrighted material.

Cover Image © Calek/Shutterstock.com.

LIBRARY OF CONGRESS CATALOGING-IN-PUBLICATION DATA

Birth control / Noël Merino, book editor.
    pages cm. -- (Teen rights and freedoms)
    Includes bibliographical references and index.
    ISBN 978-0-7377-6994-4 (hardback)
    1. Birth control--Juvenile literature. 2. Teenagers--Sexual behavior--Juvenile literature. 3. Sex instruction. I. Merino, Noël, editor of compilation.
    HQ766.8.B573 2014
    363.9′6--dc23
                                                        2013035642

3817900073853 2
Apple 8/14

Printed in the United States of America
1 2 3 4 5 6 7 18 17 16 15 14

Contents

The US Supreme Court extends the right to privacy regarding the use of contraception to all adults.

An attorney argues that laws requiring parental consent or parental notification for a minor's abortion protect the well-being of minors and the rights of parents.

A birth control educator recounts his involvement in a key US Supreme Court case that upheld the right to contraceptives and supported the subsequent right to abortion.

Foreword

The notion of children and teens having rights is a relatively recent development. Early in American history, the head of the household—nearly always the father—exercised complete control over the children in the family. Children were legally considered to be the property of their parents. Over time, this view changed, as society began to acknowledge that children have rights independent of their parents, and that the law should protect young people from exploitation. By the early twentieth century, more and more social reformers focused on the welfare of children, and over the ensuing decades advocates worked to protect them from harm in the workplace, to secure public education for all, and to guarantee fair treatment for youths in the criminal justice system. Throughout the twentieth century, rights for children and teens—and restrictions on those rights—were established by Congress and reinforced by the courts. Today's courts are still defining and clarifying the rights and freedoms of young people, sometimes expanding those rights and sometimes limiting them. Some teen rights are outside the scope of public law and remain in the realm of the family, while still others are determined by school policies.

Each volume in the Teen Rights and Freedoms series focuses on a different right or freedom and offers an anthology of key essays and articles on that right or freedom and the responsibilities that come with it. Material within each volume is drawn from a diverse selection of primary and secondary sources— journals, magazines, newspapers, nonfiction books, organization newsletters, position papers, speeches, and government documents, with a particular emphasis on Supreme Court and lower court decisions. Volumes also include first-person narratives from young people and others involved in teen rights issues, such as parents and educators. The material is selected and arranged to highlight all the major social and legal controversies relating to the right or freedom under discussion. Each selection is preceded by an introduction that provides context and background. In many cases, the essays point to the difference between adult and teen rights, and why this difference exists.

Many of the volumes cover rights guaranteed under the Bill of Rights and how these rights are interpreted and protected in regard to children and teens, including freedom of speech, freedom of the press, due process, and religious rights. The scope of the series also encompasses rights or freedoms, whether real or perceived, relating to the school environment, such as electronic devices, dress, Internet policies, and privacy. Some volumes focus on the home environment, including topics such as parental control and sexuality.

Numerous features are included in each volume of Teen Rights and Freedoms:

- An annotated **table of contents** provides a brief summary of each essay in the volume and highlights court decisions and personal narratives.
- An **introduction** specific to the volume topic gives context for the right or freedom and its impact on daily life.
- A brief **chronology** offers important dates associated with the right or freedom, including landmark court cases.
- **Primary sources**—including personal narratives and court decisions—are among the varied selections in the anthology.
- **Illustrations**—including photographs, charts, graphs, tables, statistics, and maps—are closely tied to the text and chosen to help readers understand key points or concepts.

- An annotated list of **organizations to contact** presents sources of additional information on the topic.
- A **for further reading** section offers a bibliography of books, periodical articles, and Internet sources for further research.
- A comprehensive subject **index** provides access to key people, places, events, and subjects cited in the text.

Each volume of Teen Rights and Freedoms delves deeply into the issues most relevant to the lives of teens: their own rights, freedoms, and responsibilities. With the help of this series, students and other readers can explore from many angles the evolution and current expression of rights both historic and contemporary.

Introduction

In the early part of US history, there were no laws either preventing the use of birth control or protecting the right to access and use contraception. In the early nineteenth century, several states passed laws banning the distribution and use of birth control devices. In 1873 Congress passed the Comstock Act, which prohibited the use of contraceptives in areas of federal jurisdiction and prohibited the use of the US postal service to send contraceptives or information about birth control. A 1937 federal appellate court case would challenge the application of the Comstock Act by protecting any correspondence between doctor and patient, but it was not until 1965 that the US Supreme Court would first determine that the US Constitution protects the right to access and use birth control, after which it gradually expanded the types of protected birth control and expanded the population who held the right.

The Supreme Court, in *Griswold v. Connecticut* (1965), determined that states may not ban the sale of contraceptives to married couples, arguing that there is an implicit right to marital privacy constitutionally guaranteed under the Bill of Rights. The *Griswold* case struck down a Connecticut law that prohibited the use of birth control, finding that it violated the constitutional right of privacy. Justice William O. Douglas wrote that marriage was a relationship that fell within the constitutionally protected "zones of privacy." Those zones are not explicitly mentioned in the Constitution, but Douglas wrote that the right to marital privacy was implicitly guaranteed by several parts of the Constitution, including the First, Third, Fifth, Ninth, and Fourteenth Amendments, calling the right of privacy in marriage "older than the Bill of Rights." The right to marital privacy identified in *Griswold* went on to form the basis for a variety of other decisions that lifted restrictions on the distribution and use of birth control.

A few years later, in *Eisenstadt v. Baird* (1972), the court determined that the right to privacy regarding contraceptives extends to unmarried people. The court found that there was no reasonable justification for treating married and unmarried persons differently with respect to the right to privacy identified in *Griswold*. A few years later, in *Carey v. Population Services International* (1977), the court extended the freedom to access and use birth control to minors, thereby extending the right to privacy in matters of reproduction to all people, regardless of marital status or age.

Arguably the most controversial Supreme Court case on the issue of birth control, decided in between the *Eisenstadt* and *Carey* decisions, was *Roe v. Wade* (1973), in which the court determined that the right to privacy protected a woman's right to abortion. Justice Harry Blackmun, who authored the court's opinion in *Roe*, noted, "This right of privacy . . . is broad enough to encompass a woman's decision whether or not to terminate her pregnancy." The right to abortion is not absolute, however, and the court recognized that some state regulation was allowed: "We . . . conclude that the right of personal privacy includes the abortion decision, but that this right is not unqualified, and must be considered against important state interests in regulation," noting that, "at some point, the state interests as to protection of health, medical standards, and prenatal life, become dominant." Thus the court allowed that states may regulate abortion as it regulates other medical procedures in order to protect the health of the pregnant woman. Additionally, the court determined that the state's interest in protecting fetal life was not relevant until the third trimester, at which point the states could disallow abortion "except when it is necessary to preserve the life or health of the mother."

In *Planned Parenthood of Central Missouri v. Danforth* (1976), the court struck down a state law that required parental consent—without any exceptions—in order for a minor to obtain an abortion, again referencing a minor's right to privacy.

However, the court later determined that states may require parental consent or notification for a minor's abortion if there is an alternative procedure available for a minor to get permission without the involvement of parents. In *Bellotti v. Baird* (1979), the court said that a parental-consent restriction on minors' abortions is constitutional as long as there is an alternative for the minor to obtain permission from a court. In *Planned Parenthood of Southeastern Pennsylvania v. Casey* (1992), the court upheld such a law.

The Supreme Court decisions on issues of birth control illustrate how teenagers' rights differ from those of adults. Central to the difference between a teenager's right to access and use birth control and an adult's right is the fact that minors are under the care of parents or those acting as parents. Because of this, the court has allowed that states may enact restrictions that limit the abortion rights of teenagers by imposing a parental involvement requirement in order to allow parents to be informed of, or consent to, a minor's abortion. Nonetheless, the court has noted that the rights of teenagers are strong enough to require an alternative to parental involvement, mandating that states with parental consent or parental notification laws must allow pregnant minors the ability to gain consent for abortion through a judicial process.

A 2013 federal ruling on emergency contraception highlights the ongoing controversy regarding birth control for minors. Emergency contraception became available by prescription in 1999. By 2009 the prescription requirement for those seventeen and older was removed. Although in 2011 the US Food and Drug Administration recommended that emergency contraception be sold to those of all ages over the counter, Health and Human Services Secretary Kathleen Sebelius refused to allow the removal of the age restriction. In April 2013 a federal judge ordered that the age restriction be lifted. The decision is both strongly lauded and strongly opposed, illustrating the depth of controversy on the topic of teenagers and birth control.

Four decades after the US Supreme Court established the constitutional right to access and use contraception, including abortion, the issue remains contentious. Teenage birth control access is particularly controversial and competing opinions abound on restrictions for minors. By presenting the US Supreme Court's decisions on the issue of birth control and commentary on contraceptive law and policy, *Teen Rights and Freedoms: Birth Control* sheds light on how the legal understanding of birth control in the United States continues to evolve.

Chronology

1873   US Congress passes the Comstock Act, which prohibited the importation or mailing of "obscene" matter, which was said to include contraceptives and information about birth control and abortion.

1936   In *United States v. One Package of Japanese Pessaries* the US Court of Appeals determines that the Comstock Act could not limit correspondence between doctor and patient.

1965   In *Griswold v. Connecticut* the US Supreme Court first recognizes a right of freedom of intimate association, which it said guarantees a right to privacy for married couples, finding a state law prohibiting the use of contraceptives unconstitutional.

1972   In *Eisenstadt v. Baird* the US Supreme Court rules that the right to privacy protects the right of unmarried couples to use birth control.

1973   In *Roe v. Wade* the US Supreme Court determines that the right to privacy protects the right of women to choose abortion in the early stages of pregnancy.

1976   In *Planned Parenthood of Central Missouri v. Danforth* the US Supreme

Court holds that states may not require parental consent for a minor's abortion without any exceptions, striking down one of many abortion restrictions implemented by Missouri.

1977

In *Carey v. Population Services International* the US Supreme Court rules that the rights to privacy and intimate association identified in *Griswold v. Connecticut* (1965) also extend to minors, protecting their right to access contraceptives.

1979

In *Bellotti v. Baird* the US Supreme Court rules that parental consent for a minor's abortion can be required as long as there is the alternative for a judicial bypass granting permission.

1980

In *Harris v. McRae* the US Supreme Court holds that it is constitutional for federal funding of abortion through Medicaid to be restricted and that states participating in Medicaid are not required to fund medically necessary abortions.

1983

In *Akron v. Akron Center for Reproductive Health, Inc.* the US Supreme Court determines that it is unconstitutional for a state to determine that all minors under the age of fifteen are too immature to make an abortion decision without parental approval.

1990   In *Hodgson v. Minnesota* the US
Supreme Court holds that a two-parent
notice requirement is unconstitutional,
even with a judicial bypass procedure.

1992   In *Planned Parenthood of Southeastern
Pennsylvania v. Casey* the US Supreme
Court holds that states may enact abortion restrictions at any stage of pregnancy as long as such restrictions do
not constitute an undue burden.

2007   In *Gonzales v. Carhart* the US Supreme
Court holds that the Partial-Birth
Abortion Ban Act of 2003, which
restricts certain second- and third-
trimester abortions, is constitutional.

> "By the 1960s . . . popular and legal attitudes toward birth control began to change."

Laws Prohibiting Birth Control Have Gradually Been Eliminated

Gale Encyclopedia of American Law

In the following viewpoint, the history of efforts to restrict the use of birth control in the United States is explored. The author notes how the Comstock Act of 1873 was repealed gradually during the twentieth century through a series of US Supreme Court cases that determined the right to privacy-protected access to and use of contraceptive devices. These rights eventually were extended to teenagers ages sixteen and older by the court. The author notes that there are still ongoing controversies regarding birth control, especially regarding access and use by minors.

In the 1800s, temperance unions and anti-vice societies headed efforts to prohibit birth control in the United States. Anthony Comstock, the secretary of the Society for the Suppression of Vice, advocated a highly influential law passed by Congress in

"Birth Control," *Gale Encyclopedia of American Law*, vol. 2, ed. Donna Batten, Gale, 2010, pp. 40, 42–43. Copyright © 2011 Cengage Learning.

Margaret Sanger was a pioneer of the birth control movement and founder of Planned Parenthood. Her efforts spearheaded the ease of birth control restrictions in the United States. © Everett Collection Inc./Alamy.

1873. It was titled the Act for the Suppression of Trade in, and Circulation of Obscene Literature and Articles of Immoral Use, but known popularly as the Comstock Law or Comstock Act. The Comstock Act prohibited the use of the mail system to transmit obscene materials or articles addressing or for use in the prevention of conception, including information on birth control methods or birth control devices as well as birth control devices themselves.

Soon after the federal government passed the Comstock Act, more than half of the states passed similar laws. All but two of the remaining states already had laws banning the sale, distribution, or advertising of contraceptives. Connecticut had a law that prohibited even the *use* of contraceptives; it was passed with little or no consideration for its enforceability.

Early Advocates of Birth Control

Despite popular opposition, birth control had its advocates, including Margaret Sanger. In 1916 Sanger opened in New York City the first birth control clinic in the United States. For doing so, she and her sister Ethel Byrne, who worked with her, were prosecuted under the state's version of the Comstock Law. Both were convicted and sentenced to thirty days in a workhouse.

After serving her sentence, Sanger continued to attack the Comstock Act. She established the National Committee for Federal Legislation for Birth Control, headquartered in Washington, D.C., and proposed the *doctor's bill*. This bill advocated change in the government's policy toward birth control, citing the numerous instances in which women had died owing to illegal abortions and unwanted pregnancies. The bill was defeated, due, in part, to opposition from the Catholic Church and other religious groups.

But when the issue of Sanger's sending birth control devices through the mail to a doctor was pressed in *United States v. One Package* (S.D.N.Y. 1936), the court ruled that the Comstock Act was not concerned with preventing distribution of items that might save the life or promote the well-being of a doctor's patients. Sanger had sought to challenge the Comstock Act by breaking it and sending contraception in the mail. Her efforts were victorious and the exception was made. The doctor to whom Sanger had sent the device was granted its possession.

Sanger furthered her role in reforming attitudes toward birth control by founding the Planned Parenthood Federation of America in 1942. Planned Parenthood merged previously existing birth control federations and promoted a range of birth control options. In the 1950s, Sanger supported the work of Dr. Gregory Pincus, whose research eventually produced the revolutionary birth control pill.

The Comstock Act Is Repealed

By the 1960s, partly as a result of Sanger's efforts, popular and legal attitudes toward birth control began to change. The case of *Griswold v. Connecticut* (1965), loosened the restrictions of the Comstock Act. When the Planned Parenthood League of Connecticut opened in 1961, its executive director, Estelle Griswold, faced charges of violating Connecticut's ban on the use of contraceptives.

A divided Supreme Court overturned Griswold's conviction with a ground-breaking opinion that established a constitutional right to marital privacy. The Court threw out the underlying Connecticut statute, which prohibited both using contraception and assisting or counseling others in its use. The majority opinion, authored by Justice William O. Douglas, looked briefly at a series of prior cases in which the Court had found rights not specifically enumerated in the Constitution—for example, the right of freedom of association, which the Court has said is protected by the First Amendment, even though that phrase is not used there. Douglas concluded that various guarantees contained in the Bill of Rights' Amendments One, Three, Four, Five, Nine, along with Amendment Fourteen, create "zones of privacy," which include a right of marital privacy. The Connecticut

Section One of the Comstock Act of 1873

Be it enacted . . . that whoever, within the District of Columbia or any of the Territories of the United States . . . shall sell, or lend, or give away, or in any manner exhibit, or shall offer to sell, or to lend, or to give away, or in any manner to exhibit, or shall otherwise publish or offer to publish in any manner, or shall have in his possession, for any such purpose or purposes, any obscene book, pamphlet, paper, writing, advertisement, circular, print, picture, drawing or other representation, figure, or image on or of paper or other material, or any cast, instrument, or other article of an immoral nature, or any drug or medicine, or any article whatever, for the prevention of conception, or for causing unlawful abortion, or shall advertise the same for sale, or shall write or print, or cause to be written or printed, any card, circular, book, pamphlet, advertisement, or notice of any kind, stating when, where, how, or of whom, or by what means, any of the articles in this section hereinbefore mentioned, can be purchased or obtained, or shall manufacture, draw, or print, or in any wise make any of such articles, shall be deemed guilty of a misdemeanor, and, on conviction thereof . . . he shall be imprisoned at hard labor in the penitentiary for not less than six months nor more than five years for each offense, or fined not less than one hundred dollars nor more than two thousand dollars, with costs of court.

statute, which could allow police officers to search a marital bedroom for evidence of contraception, was held unconstitutional; the government did not have a right to make such intrusions into the marital relationship.

The other branches of the government followed the Court's lead. President Lyndon B. Johnson endorsed public funding for family planning services in 1966, and the federal government began to subsidize birth control services for low-income families. In 1970 President Richard M. Nixon signed the Family Planning

Services and Population Research Act. This act supported activities related to population research and family planning.

More and more, the Comstock Act came to be seen as part of a former era, until, in 1971, the essential components of it were repealed. But this repeal was not necessarily followed in all the states. In the 1972 case of *Eisenstadt v. Baird*, the Court struck down a Massachusetts law still on the books that allowed distribution of contraceptives to married couples only. The Court held that the Massachusetts law denied single persons equal protection, in violation of the Fourteenth Amendment.

Birth Control Remains Controversial

In the 1977 case of *Carey v. Population Services International*, the Supreme Court continued to expand constitutional protections in the area of birth control. The Court imposed a strict standard of review for a New York law that it labeled "defective." The law had prohibited anyone but physicians from distributing contraceptives to minors under sixteen years of age. The law had also prohibited anyone but licensed pharmacists from distributing contraceptives to persons over sixteen. *Carey* allowed makers of contraceptives more freedom to distribute and sell their products to teens.

Throughout the 1990s, cases were brought in a number of jurisdictions in which parents sought to prohibit the distribution of condoms and other forms of birth control in schools to unemancipated minor students without the consent of a parent or guardian. Although some jurisdictions held that such birth control distribution programs violated the parents' due process rights, other jurisdictions upheld the privacy rights of such minors and found the programs to be constitutional.

More controversy arose after women gained access to RU-486, the so-called morning-after pill and later generations of emergency contraceptives, which are high-dosage birth control pills designed to be taken shortly after unprotected intercourse has taken place. Emergency contraception continues to be opposed by antiabortion groups on the ground that it is another form of abortion. However, in 2006 the FDA [US Food and Drug Administration] approved the sale of the morning after pill without a prescription to women 18 and older. In 2009, the FDA approved the sale of the pill without a prescription to 17-year old women as well.

Conservative gains in state legislatures from 2000 to 2006 strengthened the position of groups opposing abortion and reproductive rights. In addition to continuing to battle for the right to require parental consent for contraceptive services to minors both in schools and community health clinics, a number of conservative groups supported abstinence-only sexuality education classes in schools. While some proponents wanted to make such classes optional and were willing to have them taught alongside traditional courses that discuss various methods of birth control, other adherents sought to have these classes taught in place of the traditional courses. With the election of Barack Obama in 2008 and the subsequent congressional discussion of healthcare reform, the debate continued over abortion and the federal role in funding medical insurance that may or may not include covering the cost of having an abortion.

"More than 99% of women aged 15–44 who have ever had sexual intercourse have used at least one contraceptive method."

Contraceptive Use in the United States

Guttmacher Institute

In the following viewpoint, the Guttmacher Institute argues that the vast majority of sexually active women at risk of unintended pregnancy use birth control, including teenagers. The Guttmacher Institute contends that contraceptive use has broad benefits beyond prevention of pregnancy and claims that the two most commonly used contraceptives are the pill and female sterilization. The Guttmacher Institute notes that birth control is expensive and is often paid for by government programs and health insurance. The Guttmacher Institute is a nonprofit organization that seeks to advance sexual and reproductive health and rights through research, policy analysis, and public education.

Who Needs Contraceptives?

- There are 62 million U.S. women in their childbearing years (15–44). Those who are sexually active and do not want to

Guttmacher Institute, "Contraceptive Use in the United States," July 2012, pp. 1–4.

become pregnant, but could become pregnant if they and their partners fail to use a contraceptive method, are at risk of unintended pregnancy.

- Forty-three million women of childbearing age (69%) are at risk of unintended pregnancy.

- Thirty-one percent of women of reproductive age do not need a contraceptive method because they are infertile; are pregnant, postpartum or trying to become pregnant; have never had intercourse; or are not sexually active.

- Couples who do not use any method of contraception have an approximately 85% chance of experiencing a pregnancy over the course of a year.

- The typical U.S. woman wants only two children. To achieve this goal, she must use contraceptives for roughly three decades.

Who Uses Contraceptives?

- More than 99% of women aged 15–44 who have ever had sexual intercourse have used at least one contraceptive method.

- The proportion of all women of reproductive age who are currently using a contraceptive method increased from 56% in 1982 to 64% in 1995. It declined to 62% in 2002 and remained at that level in 2006–2008.

- Among women who are at risk of unintended pregnancy, 89% are currently using contraceptives.

- About one in 10 women at risk of unintended pregnancy are currently not using any contraceptive method. The proportion is highest among 15–19-year-olds (19%) and lowest among women aged 40–44 (8%).

- Eighty-four percent of black women who are at risk of unintended pregnancy currently use a contraceptive method, compared with 91% of their Hispanic and white peers, and 92% of Asian women.

- A smaller proportion of at-risk women who do not have a high school diploma than of those with at least a bachelor's degree are currently using a contraceptive method (89% vs. 92%).
- Ninety-two percent of at-risk women living at 300% or more of the federal poverty line are currently using contraceptives, compared with 88% among those living at 0–149% of poverty.
- A much higher proportion of married than of never-married women use a contraceptive method (79% vs. 39%). This is largely because married women are more likely to be sexually active. But even among those at risk of unintended pregnancy, contraceptive use is higher among currently married women than among never-married women (93% vs. 82%).
- The proportion not using a method is more than twice as high among at-risk never-married women who are not cohabiting as among at-risk married women (18% vs. 7%).
- Ninety-three percent of at-risk mothers with two children and 86% of at-risk women with no children use contraceptives.
- Contraceptive use is common among women of all religious denominations. Some 68% of Catholics who are at risk, 73% of Mainline Protestants and 74% of Evangelicals use a highly effective method (i.e., sterilization, the pill or another hormonal method, or the IUD).
- Only 2% of at-risk Catholic women rely on natural family planning; the proportion is the same even among those women who attend church once a month or more.
- More than four in 10 at-risk Evangelicals (41%) rely on male or female sterilization, the greatest proportion among religious groups.
- Knowledge about contraceptive methods is a strong predictor of use among young adults: Among unmarried women aged 18–29, for each correct response on a contraceptive knowledge scale, the odds of currently using a hormonal

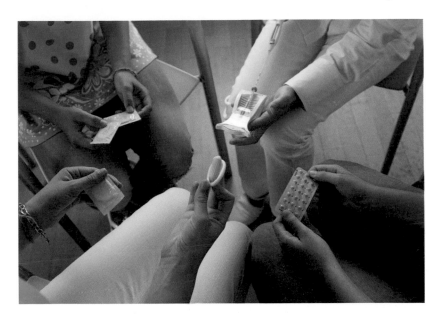

A gynecologist informs teenage girls about various types of contraception. Eighty-one percent of teen girls at risk of unintended pregnancy use contraception. © Ute Grabowsky/photothek images UG/Alamy.

or long-acting reversible method increased by 17%, and of using no method decreased by 17%.

Teen Contraceptive Use

- Among teenage women who are at risk of unintended pregnancy, 81% are currently using a contraceptive method.
- Teenagers who do not use a contraceptive method at first sex have twice as high odds of becoming teen mothers as those who use a method.
- Among sexually experienced teenagers, 78% of women and 85% of men used contraceptives the first time they had sex. Eighty-six percent and 93%, respectively, did so the last time they had sex.
- The male condom is the most commonly used method at first sex and at most recent sex among both teenage men and women.

CONTRACEPTIVE METHOD CHOICE

Contraceptive Method Use Among US Women, 2006–2008

Method	Number of Users	Percentage of Users
Pill	10,700,000	28.0
Tubal sterilization	10,400,000	27.1
Male condom	6,200,000	16.1
Vasectomy	3,800,000	9.9
IUD	2,100,000	5.5
Withdrawal	2,000,000	5.2
Three-month injectable (Depo-Provera)	1,200,000	3.2
Vaginal ring (NuvaRing)	900,000	2.4
Implant (Implanon or Norplant), one-month injectable (Lunelle) or patch (Evra)	400,000	1.1
Periodic abstinence (calendar)	300,000	0.9
Other*	200,000	0.4
Periodic abstinence (natural family planning)	100,000	0.2
Diaphragm	†	†
TOTAL	38,214,000	100.0

* Includes emergency contraception, female condom (or vaginal pouch), foam, cervical cap, Today sponge, suppository or insert, and jelly or cream (without diaphragm). †Figure does not meet standards of reliability or precision.

Taken from: Guttmacher Institute, "Contraceptive Use in the United States," July 2012. www.guttmacher.org.

- Of the 2.9 million teenage women who use contraceptives, 54% rely on the pill.
- For more information on teens, see Facts on American Teens' Sexual and Reproductive Health.

The Broad Benefits of Contraceptive Use

- Family planning has well-documented benefits for mothers, newborns, families and communities. Pregnancies that occur too early or too late in a woman's life, or that are spaced too closely, negatively affect maternal health and increase the risk of prematurity and low birth weight.
- Women use contraceptives to have healthier pregnancies, and couples use them to help time and space births, and achieve their desired family size.
- When used correctly, modern contraceptives are extremely effective at preventing pregnancy. The two-thirds of U.S. women at risk of unintended pregnancy who practice contraception consistently and correctly account for only 5% of unintended pregnancies.
- Many hormonal methods—the pill, vaginal ring, patch, implant and IUD—offer a number of health benefits in addition to contraceptive effectiveness.
- The most common reason women use oral contraceptives is to prevent pregnancy; however, 58% of pill users also cite noncontraceptive health benefits as reasons for using the method. These include treatment for excessive menstrual bleeding, menstrual pain and acne.
- Fourteen percent of oral contraceptive users—1.5 million women—rely on this method exclusively for noncontraceptive purposes.
- Some 762,000 women who have never had sex use the pill, and they do so almost exclusively for noncontraceptive reasons.

- When asked all of the reasons they use the pill, 82% of teen women cite noncontraceptive purposes, and 67% birth control. Moreover, 33% of teen pill users report using the pill solely for noncontraceptive purposes.

Which Methods Do Women Use?

- Sixty-three percent of women who practice contraception use nonpermanent methods, primarily hormonal methods (the pill, patch, implant, injectable and vaginal ring), the IUD and condoms. The rest rely on female or male sterilization.
- The pill and female sterilization have been the two most commonly used methods since 1982.
- Reliance on female sterilization varies among population subgroups. It is most common among blacks and Hispanics, women aged 35 or older, never-married women, women with two or more children, women living below 150% of the federal poverty level and women with less than a college education.
- The pill is the method most widely used by whites, women in their teens and 20s, cohabiting women, childless women and college graduates.
- As of 2009, 8.5% of women using contraceptives rely on long-acting reversible methods (the implant and the IUD). In 2002, this proportion was 2.4%.
- IUDs and implants are used most by women aged 25–39, married and cohabiting women, women covered by Medicaid, and women with no religious affiliation.
- Most of the women who use long-acting reversible methods rely on IUDs (nearly 8% of women use the IUD and less than 1% use the implant).
- Some 6.2 million women rely on the male condom. Condom use is especially common among teens and women in their 20s, women with one or no children, and women with at least a college education.

- The proportion of women using contraceptives who relied on condoms decreased from 20% to 16% between 1995 and 2006–2008.
- Some 8% of women of reproductive age use dual contraceptive methods (most often the condom combined with another method).
- The proportion of contraceptive users relying on withdrawal increased between 2002 and 2006–2008, from 4% to 5%.

Emergency Contraception

- Use of emergency contraceptive pills is a way to prevent pregnancy after unprotected sex or contraceptive failure. The pills consist of a concentrated dosage of one or more of the same hormones found in birth control pills, and they have no effect on an established pregnancy.
- Three products currently on the market (Plan B, Plan B One-Step and Next Choice) are effective when taken within 72 hours after unprotected sex (though they are decreasingly effective up to five days). A fourth product (ella) is effective for up to five days.
- Individuals younger than 17 need a prescription for emergency contraceptives, while older women and men do not. However, ella is available only by prescription.
- One in 10 women of reproductive age have used emergency contraception. Women aged 18–29, the age-group at greatest risk for unintended pregnancy, are more likely than other women to have used this backup method.
- Nonhormonal, copper IUDs, inserted up to five days after unprotected intercourse, can also act as emergency contraception.

Who Pays for Contraception?

- The costs of contraceptive services and supplies can be considerable. The most effective, long-acting methods can cost hundreds of dollars up front. Costs even for methods that are relatively inexpensive on an individual basis (such as condoms) can add up to substantial amounts over a year, much less the 30 years that the typical woman spends trying to avoid pregnancy.

- The federal and state governments provide funding for family planning services and supplies to help women meet these challenges. In 2008, an estimated 17.4 million women were in need of publicly funded services and supplies because they either had an income below 250% of the federal poverty level or were younger than 20 (and are assumed to have a low personal income).

- For more information on these services, see Facts on Publicly Funded Contraceptive Services in the United States.

- Millions of U.S. women rely on private insurance coverage to help them afford contraceptive services and supplies. Nine in 10 employer-based insurance plans cover a full range of prescription contraceptives; this proportion is three times that of just a decade ago.

- As of July 2012, some 28 states have laws in place requiring insurers that cover prescription drugs in general to cover the full range of FDA-approved contraceptive drugs and devices.

- Federal employees are guaranteed insurance coverage for contraceptives.

- Under the Affordable Care Act, a designated list of preventive services must be covered, without out-of-pocket costs to the consumer, by all private health plans written on or after August 1, 2012. Those services include provision of all FDA-approved contraceptive methods, along with sterilization procedures and contraceptive counseling to all women.

> "We deal with a right of privacy older
> than the Bill of Rights—older than our
> political parties, older than our school
> system."

The Right to Privacy Protects Marital Use of Birth Control

The Supreme Court's Decision

William O. Douglas

In the following viewpoint, US Supreme Court Justice William O. Douglas reverses a lower court decision that convicted two medical center workers for violating a Connecticut law that forbade any person from assisting another in getting birth control. Douglas found that the Connecticut law violated the constitutional right to privacy, which protects marital decisions regarding contraception. Douglas was appointed to the US Supreme Court by President Franklin D. Roosevelt in 1939 and served for more than thirty-six years, holding the record for the longest continuous service on the court.

Appellant [Estelle] Griswold is Executive Director of the Planned Parenthood League of Connecticut. Appellant [C. Lee] Buxton is a licensed physician and a professor at the Yale Medical School who served as Medical Director for the League

William O. Douglas, Majority opinion, *Griswold v. Connecticut*, US Supreme Court, June 7, 1965.

Estelle Griswold, executive director of the Planned Parenthood League of Connecticut, stands in 1963 in front of a New Haven center that was closed for advising married couples about contraception. In Griswold v. Connecticut *(1965), the US Supreme Court found that married couples have the right to access birth control.* © Lee Lockwood/Time & Life Pictures/Getty Images.

at its Center in New Haven—a center open and operating from November 1 to November 10, 1961, when appellants were arrested.

The Conviction of the Appellants

They gave information, instruction, and medical advice to *married persons* as to the means of preventing conception. They examined the wife and prescribed the best contraceptive device or material for her use. Fees were usually charged, although some couples were serviced free.

The statutes whose constitutionality is involved in this appeal are §§ 53-32 and 54-196 of the General Statutes of Connecticut (1958 rev.). The former provides:

> Any person who uses any drug, medicinal article or instrument for the purpose of preventing conception shall be fined not less than fifty dollars or imprisoned not less than sixty days nor more than one year or be both fined and imprisoned.

Section 54-196 provides:

> Any person who assists, abets, counsels, causes, hires or commands another to commit any offense may be prosecuted and punished as if he were the principal offender.

The appellants were found guilty as accessories and fined $100 each, against the claim that the accessory statute, as so applied, violated the Fourteenth Amendment. . . .

The Importance of Peripheral Rights

We are met with a wide range of questions that implicate the Due Process Clause of the Fourteenth Amendment. . . . We do not sit as a super-legislature to determine the wisdom, need, and propriety of laws that touch economic problems, business affairs, or social conditions. This law, however, operates directly on an intimate relation of husband and wife and their physician's role in one aspect of that relation.

The association of people is not mentioned in the Constitution nor in the Bill of Rights. The right to educate a child in a school of the parents' choice—whether public or private or parochial—is also not mentioned. Nor is the right to study any particular subject or any foreign language. Yet the First Amendment has been construed to include certain of those rights.

By *Pierce v. Society of Sisters* [1925] the right to educate one's children as one chooses is made applicable to the States by the force of the First and Fourteenth Amendments. By *Meyer v. Nebraska* [1923] the same dignity is given the right to study the German language in a private school. In other words, the State may not, consistently with the spirit of the First Amendment, contract the spectrum of available knowledge. The right of freedom of speech and press includes not only the right to utter or to print, but the right to distribute, the right to receive, the right to read and freedom of inquiry, freedom of thought, and freedom to teach—indeed, the freedom of the entire university community. Without those peripheral rights, the specific rights would be less secure. And so we reaffirm the principle of the *Pierce* and the *Meyer* cases.

In *NAACP v. Alabama* [1958] we protected the "freedom to associate and privacy in one's associations," noting that freedom of association was a peripheral First Amendment right. Disclosure of membership lists of a constitutionally valid association, we held, was invalid

> as entailing the likelihood of a substantial restraint upon the exercise by petitioner's members of their right to freedom of association.

In other words, the First Amendment has a penumbra where privacy is protected from governmental intrusion. In like context, we have protected forms of "association" that are not political in the customary sense, but pertain to the social, legal, and economic benefit of the members. In *Schware v. Board of Bar Examiners* [1957] we held it not permissible to bar a law-

The Significance of *Griswold v. Connecticut*

Griswold [v. Connecticut (1965)] was the first in a series of constitutional cases dealing with the rights to privacy and to abortion, which set the stage for debate over fundamental rights jurisprudence. As a result of this decision, the Court was criticized for its protection of rights not explicitly granted by the Constitution as fundamental rights. This case demonstrated that in the proper context, the Court was willing to go beyond the text in protecting what was established by the Constitution as fundamental. It viewed the Constitution as a living document, for adaptation when the needs of society changed and its technology advanced.

Richard A. Leiter and Roy M. Mersky, "Case Title: Griswold v. Connecticut," pp. 769–773 in Landmark Supreme Court Cases: The Most Influential Decisions of the Supreme Court of the United States. *New York: Facts On File, 2012.*

yer from practice because he had once been a member of the Communist Party. The man's "association with that Party" was not shown to be "anything more than a political faith in a political party," and was not action of a kind proving bad moral character.

Those cases involved more than the "right of assembly"—a right that extends to all, irrespective of their race or ideology. The right of "association," like the right of belief, is more than the right to attend a meeting; it includes the right to express one's attitudes or philosophies by membership in a group or by affiliation with it or by other lawful means. Association in that context is a form of expression of opinion, and, while it is not expressly included in the First Amendment, its existence is necessary in making the express guarantees fully meaningful.

The Right to Privacy

The foregoing cases suggest that specific guarantees in the Bill of Rights have penumbras, formed by emanations from those guarantees that help give them life and substance. Various guarantees create zones of privacy. The right of association contained in the penumbra of the First Amendment is one, as we have seen. The Third Amendment, in its prohibition against the quartering of soldiers "in any house" in time of peace without the consent of the owner, is another facet of that privacy. The Fourth Amendment explicitly affirms the "right of the people to be secure in their persons, houses, papers, and effects, against unreasonable searches and seizures." The Fifth Amendment, in its Self-Incrimination Clause, enables the citizen to create a zone of privacy which government may not force him to surrender to his detriment. The Ninth Amendment provides: "The enumeration in the Constitution, of certain rights, shall not be construed to deny or disparage others retained by the people."

The Fourth and Fifth Amendments were described in *Boyd v. United States* [1886] as protection against all governmental invasions "of the sanctity of a man's home and the privacies of life." We recently referred in *Mapp v. Ohio* [1961] to the Fourth Amendment as creating a "right to privacy, no less important than any other right carefully and particularly reserved to the people."

We have had many controversies over these penumbral rights of "privacy and repose." These cases bear witness that the right of privacy which presses for recognition here is a legitimate one.

The present case, then, concerns a relationship lying within the zone of privacy created by several fundamental constitutional guarantees. And it concerns a law which, in forbidding the use of contraceptives, rather than regulating their manufacture or sale, seeks to achieve its goals by means having a maximum destructive impact upon that relationship. Such a law cannot stand in light of the familiar principle, so often applied by this Court, that a governmental purpose to control or prevent activities constitutionally subject to state regulation may not be achieved by means which sweep unnecessarily broadly and thereby invade the area of protected freedoms. [*NAACP v. Alabama* (1958)]

Would we allow the police to search the sacred precincts of marital bedrooms for telltale signs of the use of contraceptives? The very idea is repulsive to the notions of privacy surrounding the marriage relationship.

We deal with a right of privacy older than the Bill of Rights— older than our political parties, older than our school system. Marriage is a coming together for better or for worse, hopefully enduring, and intimate to the degree of being sacred. It is an association that promotes a way of life, not causes; a harmony in living, not political faiths; a bilateral loyalty, not commercial or social projects. Yet it is an association for as noble a purpose as any involved in our prior decisions.

> "It is the right of the individual,
> married or single, to be free from
> unwarranted governmental intrusion
> into matters . . . [such] as the decision
> whether to bear or beget a child."

The Right to Privacy in Contraception Extends to Unmarried Individuals

The Supreme Court's Decision

William J. Brennan Jr.

In the following viewpoint, US Supreme Court Justice William J. Brennan Jr. determines that the constitutional right to privacy protects the rights of all adults—whether married or unmarried—to use contraception. The state's justifications for the laws treating unmarried persons different from married persons were considered and rejected as a violation of the Equal Protection Clause of the Fourteenth Amendment. The court concluded that single people, as well as married couples, have a right to privacy protecting their use of birth control. William J. Brennan Jr. was a justice of the US Supreme Court from 1956 to 1990 and is considered to have been one of the more influential justices to have sat on the court.

Appellee William Baird was convicted at a bench trial in the Massachusetts Superior Court under Massachusetts

William J. Brennan Jr., Majority opinion, *Eisenstadt v. Baird*, US Supreme Court, March 22, 1972.

General Laws Ann., c. 272, 21, first, for exhibiting contraceptive articles in the course of delivering a lecture on contraception to a group of students at Boston University and, second, for giving a young woman a package of Emko vaginal foam at the close of his address. The Massachusetts Supreme Judicial Court unanimously set aside the conviction for exhibiting contraceptives on the ground that it violated Baird's First Amendment rights, but by a four-to-three vote sustained the conviction for giving away the foam. . . .

Examining the Massachusetts Law

Massachusetts General Laws Ann., c. 272, 21, under which Baird was convicted, provides a maximum five-year term of imprisonment for "whoever . . . gives away . . . any drug, medicine, instrument or article whatever for the prevention of conception," except as authorized in 21A. Under 21A, "[a] registered physician may administer to or prescribe for any married person drugs or articles intended for the prevention of pregnancy or conception. [And a] registered pharmacist actually engaged in the business of pharmacy may furnish such drugs or articles to any married person presenting a prescription from a registered physician." As interpreted by the State Supreme Judicial Court, these provisions make it a felony for anyone, other than a registered physician or pharmacist acting in accordance with the terms of 21A, to dispense any article with the intention that it be used for the prevention of conception. The statutory scheme distinguishes among three distinct classes of distributees—first, married persons may obtain contraceptives to prevent pregnancy, but only from doctors or druggists on prescription; second, single persons may not obtain contraceptives from anyone to prevent pregnancy; and, third, married or single persons may obtain contraceptives from anyone to prevent, not pregnancy, but the spread of disease. This construction of state law is, of course, binding on us.

The legislative purposes that the statute is meant to serve are not altogether clear. In *Commonwealth v. Baird* [1969], the

Section One of the Fourteenth Amendment to the US Constitution

All persons born or naturalized in the United States, and subject to the jurisdiction thereof, are citizens of the United States and of the state wherein they reside. No state shall make or enforce any law which shall abridge the privileges or immunities of citizens of the United States; nor shall any state deprive any person of life, liberty, or property, without due process of law; nor deny to any person within its jurisdiction the equal protection of the laws.

Supreme Judicial Court noted only the State's interest in protecting the health of its citizens: "[T]he prohibition in 21," the court declared, "is directly related to" the State's goal of "preventing the distribution of articles designed to prevent conception which may have undesirable, if not dangerous, physical consequences." In a subsequent decision, *Sturgis v. Attorney General* (1970), the court, however, found "a second and more compelling ground for upholding the statute"—namely, to protect morals through "regulating the private sexual lives of single persons." The Court of Appeals, for reasons that will appear, did not consider the promotion of health or the protection of morals through the deterrence of fornication to be the legislative aim. Instead, the court concluded that the statutory goal was to limit contraception in and of itself—a purpose that the court held conflicted "with fundamental human rights" under *Griswold v. Connecticut* (1965), where this Court struck down Connecticut's prohibition against the use of contraceptives as an unconstitutional infringement of the right of marital privacy.

We agree that the goals of deterring premarital sex and regulating the distribution of potentially harmful articles cannot reasonably be regarded as legislative aims of 21 and 21A. And we hold that the statute, viewed as a prohibition on contraception per se, violates the rights of single persons under the Equal Protection Clause of the Fourteenth Amendment. . . .

The Equal Protection Clause

The basic principles governing application of the Equal Protection Clause of the Fourteenth Amendment are familiar. As the Chief Justice only recently explained in *Reed v. Reed* (1971):

> In applying that clause, this Court has consistently recognized that the Fourteenth Amendment does not deny to States the power to treat different classes of persons in different ways. The Equal Protection Clause of that amendment does, however, deny to States the power to legislate that different treatment be accorded to persons placed by a statute into different classes on the basis of criteria wholly unrelated to the objective of that statute. A classification 'must be reasonable, not arbitrary, and must rest upon some ground of difference having a fair and substantial relation to the object of the legislation, so that all persons similarly circumstanced shall be treated alike.' [*Royster Guano Co. v. Virginia* (1920)].

The question for our determination in this case is whether there is some ground of difference that rationally explains the different treatment accorded married and unmarried persons under Massachusetts General Laws Ann., c. 272, 21 and 21A. For the reasons that follow, we conclude that no such ground exists.

The Goal of Deterring Premarital Sex

First. Section 21 stems from Mass. Stat. 1879, c. 159, 1, which prohibited, without exception, distribution of articles intended to be used as contraceptives. In *Commonwealth v. Allison* (1917), the Massachusetts Supreme Judicial Court explained that the law's "plain purpose is to protect purity, to preserve chastity, to encourage continence and self-restraint, to defend the sanctity of the home, and thus to engender in the State and nation a virile and virtuous race of men and women." Although the State clearly abandoned that purpose with the enactment of 21A, at least insofar as the illicit sexual activities of married persons are concerned, the court reiterated in *Sturgis v. Attorney General* that the object of the legislation is to discourage premarital sexual intercourse. Conceding that the State could, consistently with the Equal Protection Clause, regard the problems of extramarital and premarital sexual relations as "[e]vils . . . of different dimensions and proportions, requiring different remedies," [*Williamson v. Lee Optical Co.* (1955)], we cannot agree that the deterrence of premarital sex may reasonably be regarded as the purpose of the Massachusetts law.

It would be plainly unreasonable to assume that Massachusetts has prescribed pregnancy and the birth of an unwanted child as punishment for fornication, which is a misdemeanor under Massachusetts General Laws Ann., c. 272, 18. Aside from the scheme of values that assumption would attribute to the State, it is abundantly clear that the effect of the ban on distribution of contraceptives to unmarried persons has at best a marginal relation to the proffered objective. What Mr. Justice [Arthur] Goldberg said in *Griswold v. Connecticut*, concerning the effect of Connecticut's prohibition on the use of contraceptives in discouraging extramarital sexual relations, is equally applicable here. "The rationality of this justification is dubious, particularly in light of the admitted widespread availability to all persons in the State of Connecticut, unmarried as well as married, of birth-control devices for the prevention of disease, as distinguished from the prevention of conception." Like Connecticut's laws, 21 and 21A do not at all regulate the distribution of contraceptives when they are to be used to prevent, not pregnancy, but the spread of disease. Nor, in making contraceptives available to married persons without regard to their intended use, does Massachusetts attempt to deter married persons from engaging in illicit sexual relations with unmarried persons. Even on the assumption that the fear of pregnancy operates as a deterrent to fornication, the Massachusetts statute is thus so riddled with exceptions that deterrence of premarital sex cannot reasonably be regarded as its aim.

Moreover, 21 and 21A on their face have a dubious relation to the State's criminal prohibition on fornication. As the Court of Appeals explained, "Fornication is a misdemeanor [in Massachusetts], entailing a thirty dollar fine, or three months in jail. Violation of the present statute is a felony, punishable by five years in prison. We find it hard to believe that the legislature adopted a statute carrying a five-year penalty for its possible, obviously by no means fully effective, deterrence of the commission of a ninety-day misdemeanor." Even conceding the legislature a full measure of discretion in fashioning means to prevent fornication, and recognizing that the State may seek to deter prohibited conduct by punishing more severely those who facilitate than those who actually engage in its commission, we, like the Court of Appeals, cannot believe that in this instance Massachusetts has chosen to expose the aider and abetter who simply gives away a contraceptive to 20 times the 90-day sentence of the offender himself. The very terms of the State's criminal statutes, coupled with the *de minimis* [insignificant] effect of 21 and 21A in deterring fornication, thus compel the conclusion that such deterrence cannot reasonably be taken as the purpose of the ban on distribution of contraceptives to unmarried persons.

The Goal of Protecting Health

Second. Section 21A was added to the Massachusetts General Laws by Stat. 1966, c. 265, 1. The Supreme Judicial Court in *Commonwealth v. Baird* held that the purpose of the amendment was to serve the health needs of the community by regulating the distribution of potentially harmful articles. It is plain that Massachusetts had no such purpose in mind before the enactment of 21A. As the Court of Appeals remarked, "Consistent with the fact that the statute was contained in a chapter dealing with 'Crimes Against Chastity, Morality, Decency and Good Order,' it was cast only in terms of morals. A physician was forbidden to prescribe contraceptives even when needed for the protection of health." Nor did the Court of Appeals "believe that the legislature [in enacting 21A] suddenly reversed its field and developed an interest in health. Rather, it merely made what it thought to be the precise accommodation necessary to escape the *Griswold* ruling."

Again, we must agree with the Court of Appeals. If health were the rationale of 21A, the statute would be both discriminatory and overbroad. Dissenting in *Commonwealth v. Baird*, Justices [Arthur Easterbrook] Whittemore and [Richard Ammi] Cutter stated that they saw "in 21 and 21A, read together, no public health purpose. If there is need to have a physician prescribe (and a pharmacist dispense) contraceptives, that need is as great for unmarried persons as for married persons." The Court of Appeals added: "If the prohibition [on distribution to unmarried persons] . . . is to be taken to mean that the same physician who can prescribe for married patients does not have sufficient skill to protect the health of patients who lack a marriage certificate, or who may be currently divorced, it is illogical to the point of irrationality." Furthermore, we must join the Court of Appeals in noting that not all contraceptives are potentially dangerous. As a result, if the Massachusetts statute were a health measure, it would not only invidiously discriminate against the unmarried, but also be overbroad with respect to the married, a fact that the Supreme Judicial Court itself seems to have conceded in *Sturgis v. Attorney General*, where it noted that "it may well be that certain contraceptive medication and devices constitute no hazard to health, in which event it could be argued that the statute swept too broadly in its prohibition." "In this posture," as the Court of Appeals concluded, "it is impossible to think of the statute as intended as a health measure for the unmarried, and it is almost as difficult to think of it as so intended even as to the married."

But if further proof that the Massachusetts statute is not a health measure is necessary, the argument of Justice [Jacob]

US Supreme Court Justice William J. Brennan Jr. argues that all individuals, regardless of marital status, have the right to access birth control. In Eisenstadt v. Baird *(1972), the Supreme Court ruled that a Massachusetts law that forbade unmarried individuals from using contraception violated the Fourteenth Amendment of the US Constitution.* © Consolidated News/Getty Images.

Spiegel, who also dissented in *Commonwealth v. Baird* is conclusive: "It is at best a strained conception to say that the Legislature intended to prevent the distribution of articles 'which may have undesirable, if not dangerous, physical consequences.' If that was the Legislature's goal, 21 is not required" in view of the federal and state laws already regulating the distribution of harmful drugs. We conclude, accordingly, that, despite the statute's superficial earmarks as a health measure, health, on the face of the statute, may no more reasonably be regarded as its purpose than the deterrence of premarital sexual relations.

The Goal of Promoting Morality

Third. If the Massachusetts statute cannot be upheld as a deterrent to fornication or as a health measure, may it, nevertheless, be sustained simply as a prohibition on contraception? The Court of Appeals analysis "led inevitably to the conclusion that, so far as morals are concerned, it is contraceptives per se that are considered immoral—to the extent that *Griswold* will permit such a declaration." The Court of Appeals went on to hold:

> To say that contraceptives are immoral as such, and are to be forbidden to unmarried persons who will nevertheless persist in having intercourse, means that such persons must risk for themselves an unwanted pregnancy, for the child, illegitimacy, and for society, a possible obligation of support. Such a view of morality is not only the very mirror image of sensible legislation; we consider that it conflicts with fundamental human rights. In the absence of demonstrated harm, we hold it is beyond the competency of the state.

We need not and do not, however, decide that important question in this case because, whatever the rights of the individual to access to contraceptives may be, the rights must be the same for the unmarried and the married alike.

If under *Griswold* the distribution of contraceptives to married persons cannot be prohibited, a ban on distribution to unmarried persons would be equally impermissible. It is true that in *Griswold* the right of privacy in question inhered in the marital relationship. Yet the marital couple is not an independent entity with a mind and heart of its own, but an association of two individuals each with a separate intellectual and emotional makeup. If the right of privacy means anything, it is the right of the individual, married or single, to be free from unwarranted governmental intrusion into matters so fundamentally affecting a person as the decision whether to bear or beget a child.

On the other hand, if *Griswold* is no bar to a prohibition on the distribution of contraceptives, the State could not, consistently with the Equal Protection Clause, outlaw distribution to unmarried but not to married persons. In each case the evil, as perceived by the State, would be identical, and the underinclusion would be invidious. Mr. Justice [Robert H.] Jackson, concurring in *Railway Express Agency v. New York* (1949), made the point:

> The framers of the Constitution knew, and we should not forget today, that there is no more effective practical guaranty against arbitrary and unreasonable government than to require that the principles of law which officials would impose upon a minority must be imposed generally. Conversely, nothing opens the door to arbitrary action so effectively as to allow those officials to pick and choose only a few to whom they will apply legislation and thus to escape the political retribution that might be visited upon them if larger numbers were affected. Courts can take no better measure to assure that laws will be just than to require that laws be equal in operation.

Although Mr. Justice Jackson's comments had reference to administrative regulations, the principle he affirmed has equal application to the legislation here. We hold that by providing dissimilar treatment for married and unmarried persons who are similarly situated, Massachusetts General Laws Ann., c. 272, 21 and 21A, violate the Equal Protection Clause.

"We . . . conclude that the right of
personal privacy includes the abortion
decision, but that this right is not
unqualified, and must be considered
against important state interests in
regulation."

The Right to Privacy Protects a Woman's Right to Choose Abortion

The Supreme Court's Decision

Harry Blackmun

In the following viewpoint, US Supreme Court Justice Harry Blackmun argues that the right to privacy protects a woman's right to abortion. Blackmun recounts the history of abortion laws in the United States, noting that the state laws at the time of Roe v. Wade (1973) were more restrictive than they had been in the past. He rejects three justifications for laws criminalizing abortion. Rejecting the notion of the fetus as a person, Blackmun nonetheless notes that there is a compelling interest for the state to protect fetal life after the end of the second trimester and to protect the life of the mother after the end of the first trimester, thus allowing increasing restrictions in the second and third trimesters. Blackmun served as an associate justice of the US Supreme Court from 1970 to 1994.

Harry Blackmun, Majority opinion, Roe v. Wade, US Supreme Court, January 22, 1973.

The Texas statutes that concern us here . . . make it a crime to "procure an abortion," as therein defined, or to attempt one, except with respect to "an abortion procured or attempted by medical advice for the purpose of saving the life of the mother." Similar statutes are in existence in a majority of the States.

The Constitutionality of the Texas Statutes

Jane Roe, a single woman who was residing in Dallas County, Texas, instituted this federal action in March 1970 against the District Attorney of the county. She sought a declaratory judgment that the Texas criminal abortion statutes were unconstitutional on their face, and an injunction restraining the defendant from enforcing the statutes.

Roe alleged that she was unmarried and pregnant; that she wished to terminate her pregnancy by an abortion "performed by a competent, licensed physician, under safe, clinical conditions"; that she was unable to get a "legal" abortion in Texas because her life did not appear to be threatened by the continuation of her pregnancy; and that she could not afford to travel to another jurisdiction in order to secure a legal abortion under safe conditions. She claimed that the Texas statutes were unconstitutionally vague and that they abridged her right of personal privacy, protected by the First, Fourth, Fifth, Ninth, and Fourteenth Amendments. By an amendment to her complaint, Roe purported to sue "on behalf of herself and all other women" similarly situated.

James Hubert Hallford, a licensed physician, sought and was granted leave to intervene in Roe's action. In his complaint, he alleged that he had been arrested previously for violations of the Texas abortion statutes, and that two such prosecutions were pending against him. He described conditions of patients who came to him seeking abortions, and he claimed that for many cases he, as a physician, was unable to determine whether they fell within or outside the exception recognized by Article 1196.

Norma McCorvey (left) was the "Jane Roe" in Roe v. Wade *(1973). In this landmark decision, the US Supreme Court ruled that women have the right to obtain an abortion.* © Kevin Larkin/AFP/Getty Images.

He alleged that, as a consequence, the statutes were vague and uncertain, in violation of the Fourteenth Amendment, and that they violated his own and his patients' rights to privacy in the doctor-patient relationship and his own right to practice medicine, rights he claimed were guaranteed by the First, Fourth, Fifth, Ninth, and Fourteenth Amendments. . . .

The History of Criminal Abortion Laws

The principal thrust of appellant's attack on the Texas statutes is that they improperly invade a right, said to be possessed by the pregnant woman, to choose to terminate her pregnancy. Appellant would discover this right in the concept of personal "liberty" embodied in the Fourteenth Amendment's Due Process Clause; or in personal, marital, familial, and sexual privacy said to be protected by the Bill of Rights or its penumbras; or among those rights reserved to the people by the Ninth Amendment. Before addressing this claim, we feel it desirable briefly to survey, in several aspects, the history of abortion, for such insight as that history may afford us, and then to examine the state purposes and interests behind the criminal abortion laws.

It perhaps is not generally appreciated that the restrictive criminal abortion laws in effect in a majority of States today are of relatively recent vintage. Those laws, generally proscribing abortion or its attempt at any time during pregnancy except when necessary to preserve the pregnant woman's life, are not of ancient or even of common law origin. Instead, they derive from statutory changes effected, for the most part, in the latter half of the 19th century. . . .

At the time of the adoption of our Constitution, and throughout the major portion of the 19th century, abortion was viewed with less disfavor than under most American statutes currently in effect. Phrasing it another way, a woman enjoyed a substantially broader right to terminate a pregnancy than she does in most States today. At least with respect to the early stage of pregnancy, and very possibly without such a limitation, the opportunity to make this choice was present in this country well into the 19th century. Even later, the law continued for some time to treat less punitively an abortion procured in early pregnancy. . . .

Three Justifications for Criminal Abortion Laws

Three reasons have been advanced to explain historically the enactment of criminal abortion laws in the 19th century and to justify their continued existence.

It has been argued occasionally that these laws were the product of a Victorian social concern to discourage illicit sexual conduct. Texas, however, does not advance this justification in the present case, and it appears that no court or commentator has taken the argument seriously. The appellants and *amici* [supporters] contend, moreover, that this is not a proper state purpose, at all and suggest that, if it were, the Texas statutes are overbroad in protecting it, since the law fails to distinguish between married and unwed mothers.

A second reason is concerned with abortion as a medical procedure. When most criminal abortion laws were first enacted, the procedure was a hazardous one for the woman. This was particularly true prior to the development of antisepsis. Antiseptic techniques, of course, were based on discoveries by Lister, Pasteur, and others first announced in 1867, but were not generally accepted and employed until about the turn of the century. Abortion mortality was high. Even after 1900, and perhaps until as late as the development of antibiotics in the 1940's, standard modern techniques such as dilation and curettage were not nearly so safe as they are today. Thus, it has been argued that a State's real concern in enacting a criminal abortion law was to protect the pregnant woman, that is, to restrain her from submitting to a procedure that placed her life in serious jeopardy.

Modern medical techniques have altered this situation. Appellants and various *amici* refer to medical data indicating that abortion in early pregnancy, that is, prior to the end of the first trimester, although not without its risk, is now relatively safe. Mortality rates for women undergoing early abortions, where the procedure is legal, appear to be as low as or lower than the rates for normal childbirth. Consequently, any interest of the State in protecting the woman from an inherently hazardous procedure, except when it would be equally dangerous for her to forgo it, has largely disappeared. Of course, important state interests in the areas of health and medical standards do remain. The State has a legitimate interest in seeing to it that abortion, like any other medical procedure, is performed under circumstances that insure maximum safety for the patient. This interest obviously extends at least to the performing physician and his staff, to the facilities involved, to the availability of after-care, and to adequate provision for any complication or emergency that might arise. The prevalence of high mortality rates at illegal "abortion mills" strengthens, rather than weakens, the State's interest in regulating the conditions under which abortions are performed. Moreover, the risk to the woman increases as her pregnancy continues. Thus, the State retains a definite interest in protecting the woman's own health and safety when an abortion is proposed at a late stage of pregnancy.

The third reason is the State's interest—some phrase it in terms of duty—in protecting prenatal life. Some of the argument for this justification rests on the theory that a new human life is present from the moment of conception. The State's interest and general obligation to protect life then extends, it is argued, to prenatal life. Only when the life of the pregnant mother herself is at stake, balanced against the life she carries within her, should the interest of the embryo or fetus not prevail. Logically, of course, a legitimate state interest in this area need not stand or fall on acceptance of the belief that life begins at conception or at some other point prior to live birth. In assessing the State's interest, recognition may be given to the less rigid claim that as long as at least potential life is involved, the State may assert interests beyond the protection of the pregnant woman alone. . . .

The Right of Personal Privacy

The Constitution does not explicitly mention any right of privacy. In a line of decisions, however, going back perhaps as far as *Union Pacific R. Co. v. Botsford* (1891), the Court has recognized that a right of personal privacy, or a guarantee of certain areas or zones of privacy, does exist under the Constitution. In varying contexts, the Court or individual Justices have, indeed, found at least the roots of that right in the First Amendment, in the Fourth and Fifth Amendments, in the penumbras of the Bill of Rights, in the Ninth Amendment, or in the concept of liberty guaranteed by the first section of the Fourteenth Amendment. These decisions make it clear that only personal rights that can be deemed "fundamental" or "implicit in the concept of ordered liberty" [*Palko v. Connecticut* (1937)], are included in this guarantee of personal privacy. They also make it clear that the right has some extension to activities relating to marriage, procreation, contraception, family relationships, and childrearing and education.

This right of privacy, whether it be founded in the Fourteenth Amendment's concept of personal liberty and restrictions upon state action, as we feel it is, or, as the District Court determined, in the Ninth Amendment's reservation of rights to the people, is broad enough to encompass a woman's decision whether or not to terminate her pregnancy. The detriment that the State would impose upon the pregnant woman by denying this choice altogether is apparent. Specific and direct harm medically diagnosable even in early pregnancy may be involved. Maternity, or additional offspring, may force upon the woman a distressful life and future. Psychological harm may be imminent. Mental and physical health may be taxed by child care. There is also the distress, for all concerned, associated with the unwanted child, and there is the problem of bringing a child into a family already unable, psychologically and otherwise, to care for it. In other cases, as in this one, the additional difficulties and continuing stigma of unwed motherhood may be involved. All these are factors the woman and her responsible physician necessarily will consider in consultation.

On the basis of elements such as these, appellant and some *amici* argue that the woman's right is absolute and that she is entitled to terminate her pregnancy at whatever time, in whatever way, and for whatever reason she alone chooses. With this we do not agree. Appellant's arguments that Texas either has no valid interest at all in regulating the abortion decision, or no interest strong enough to support any limitation upon the woman's sole determination, are unpersuasive. The Court's decisions recognizing a right of privacy also acknowledge that some state regulation in areas protected by that right is appropriate. As noted above, a State may properly assert important interests in safeguarding health, in maintaining medical standards, and in protecting potential life. At some point in pregnancy, these respective interests become sufficiently compelling to sustain regulation of the factors that govern the abortion decision. The privacy right involved, therefore, cannot be said to be absolute. In fact, it is not clear to us that the claim asserted by some *amici* that one has an

PUBLIC OPINION ON *ROE V. WADE*

The US Supreme Court's 1973 *Roe v. Wade* decision established a woman's constitutional right to an abortion, at least in the first three months of pregnancy. Would you like to see the Supreme Court completely overturn its *Roe v. Wade* decision, or not?

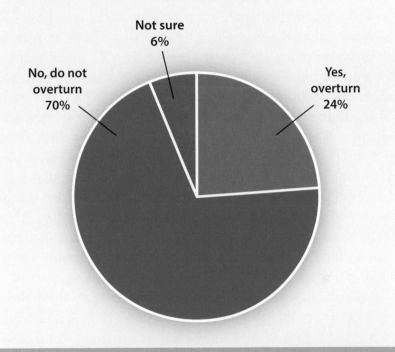

Not sure
6%

No, do not
overturn
70%

Yes,
overturn
24%

Taken from: NBC News/*Wall Street Journal* Survey, January 12–15, 2013.

unlimited right to do with one's body as one pleases bears a close relationship to the right of privacy previously articulated in the Court's decisions. The Court has refused to recognize an unlimited right of this kind in the past.

We, therefore, conclude that the right of personal privacy includes the abortion decision, but that this right is not unqualified, and must be considered against important state interests in regulation. . . .

The Status of the Fetus

The appellee and certain *amici* argue that the fetus is a "person" within the language and meaning of the Fourteenth Amendment. In support of this, they outline at length and in detail the well known facts of fetal development. If this suggestion of personhood is established, the appellant's case, of course, collapses, for the fetus' right to life would then be guaranteed specifically by the Amendment. The appellant conceded as much on reargument. On the other hand, the appellee conceded on reargument that no case could be cited that holds that a fetus is a person within the meaning of the Fourteenth Amendment.

The Constitution does not define "person" in so many words. Section 1 of the Fourteenth Amendment contains three references to "person." The first, in defining "citizens," speaks of "persons born or naturalized in the United States." The word also appears both in the Due Process Clause and in the Equal Protection Clause. "Person" is used in other places in the Constitution. . . . But in nearly all these instances, the use of the word is such that it has application only post-natally. None indicates, with any assurance, that it has any possible pre-natal application.

All this, together with our observation that, throughout the major portion of the 19th century, prevailing legal abortion practices were far freer than they are today, persuades us that the word "person," as used in the Fourteenth Amendment, does not include the unborn. This is in accord with the results reached in those few cases where the issue has been squarely presented. . . .

Texas urges that, apart from the Fourteenth Amendment, life begins at conception and is present throughout pregnancy, and that, therefore, the State has a compelling interest in protecting that life from and after conception. We need not resolve the difficult question of when life begins. When those trained in the respective disciplines of medicine, philosophy, and theology are unable to arrive at any consensus, the judiciary, at this point in the development of man's knowledge, is not in a position to speculate as to the answer. . . .

Permissible State Regulation of Abortion

In view of all this, we do not agree that, by adopting one theory of life, Texas may override the rights of the pregnant woman that are at stake. We repeat, however, that the State does have an important and legitimate interest in preserving and protecting the health of the pregnant woman, whether she be a resident of the State or a nonresident who seeks medical consultation and treatment there, and that it has still *another* important and legitimate interest in protecting the potentiality of human life. These interests are separate and distinct. Each grows in substantiality as the woman approaches term and, at a point during pregnancy, each becomes "compelling."

With respect to the State's important and legitimate interest in the health of the mother, the "compelling" point, in the light of present medical knowledge, is at approximately the end of the first trimester. This is so because of the now-established medical fact that, until the end of the first trimester mortality in abortion may be less than mortality in normal childbirth. It follows that, from and after this point, a State may regulate the abortion procedure to the extent that the regulation reasonably relates to the preservation and protection of maternal health. Examples of permissible state regulation in this area are requirements as to the qualifications of the person who is to perform the abortion; as to the licensure of that person; as to the facility in which the procedure is to be performed, that is, whether it must be a hospital or may be a clinic or some other place of less-than-hospital status; as to the licensing of the facility; and the like.

This means, on the other hand, that, for the period of pregnancy prior to this "compelling" point, the attending physician, in consultation with his patient, is free to determine, without regulation by the State, that, in his medical judgment, the patient's pregnancy should be terminated. If that decision is reached, the judgment may be effectuated by an abortion free of interference by the State.

With respect to the State's important and legitimate interest in potential life, the "compelling" point is at viability. This is so because the fetus then presumably has the capability of meaningful life outside the mother's womb. State regulation protective of fetal life after viability thus has both logical and biological justifications. If the State is interested in protecting fetal life after viability, it may go so far as to proscribe abortion during that period, except when it is necessary to preserve the life or health of the mother. . . .

To summarize and to repeat:

1. A state criminal abortion statute of the current Texas type, that excepts from criminality only a lifesaving procedure on behalf of the mother, without regard to pregnancy stage and without recognition of the other interests involved, is violative of the Due Process Clause of the Fourteenth Amendment.

    (a) For the stage prior to approximately the end of the first trimester, the abortion decision and its effectuation must be left to the medical judgment of the pregnant woman's attending physician.

    (b) For the stage subsequent to approximately the end of the first trimester, the State, in promoting its interest in the health of the mother, may, if it chooses, regulate the abortion procedure in ways that are reasonably related to maternal health.

    (c) For the stage subsequent to viability, the State in promoting its interest in the potentiality of human life may, if it chooses, regulate, and even proscribe, abortion except where it is necessary, in appropriate medical judgment, for the preservation of the life or health of the mother.

| "*The right to privacy in connection with decisions affecting procreation extends to minors, as well as to adults.*"

It Is a Violation of Minors' Right to Privacy to Restrict Access to Contraceptives

The Supreme Court's Decision

William J. Brennan Jr.

In the following viewpoint, US Supreme Court Justice William J. Brennan Jr. argues that a New York state law criminalizing the sale of birth control to minors is unconstitutional. Brennan notes that the court has recognized a right to privacy in many areas, but especially as such a right relates to whether or not to have a child. Brennan argues that although the state may sometimes impose restrictions on minors, it cannot restrict the sale of contraceptives without also violating privacy rights. Brennan was associate justice of the US Supreme Court from 1956 until his retirement in 1990.

Under New York Educ. Law § 6811 (8), it is a crime (1) for any person to sell or distribute any contraceptive of any kind to

William J. Brennan Jr., Majority opinion, *Carey v. Population Services International*, US Supreme Court, June 9, 1977.

a minor under the age of 16 years; (2) for anyone other than a licensed pharmacist to distribute contraceptives to persons 16 or over; and (3) for anyone, including licensed pharmacists, to advertise or display contraceptives. . . .

The Right of Personal Privacy

Although "[t]he Constitution does not explicitly mention any right of privacy," the Court has recognized that one aspect of the "liberty" protected by the Due Process Clause of the Fourteenth Amendment is "a right of personal privacy, or a guarantee of certain areas or zones of privacy" [*Roe v. Wade* (1973)]. . . . This right of personal privacy includes "the interest in independence in making certain kinds of important decisions" [*Whalen v. Roe* (1977)]. While the outer limits of this aspect of privacy have not been marked by the Court, it is clear that among the decisions that an individual may make without unjustified government interference are personal decisions relating to marriage, procreation, contraception, family relationships, and childrearing and education [*Roe v. Wade*].

The decision whether or not to beget or bear a child is at the very heart of this cluster of constitutionally protected choices. That decision holds a particularly important place in the history of the right of privacy, a right first explicitly recognized in an opinion holding unconstitutional a statute prohibiting the use of contraceptives, and most prominently vindicated in recent years in the contexts of contraception and abortion. This is understandable, for in a field that, by definition, concerns the most intimate of human activities and relationships, decisions whether to accomplish or to prevent conception are among the most private and sensitive.

> If the right of privacy means anything, it is the right of the individual, married or single, to be free of unwarranted governmental intrusion into matters so fundamentally affecting a person as the decision whether to bear or beget a child. [*Eisenstadt v. Baird* (1972)].

That the constitutionally protected right of privacy extends to an individual's liberty to make choices regarding contraception does not, however, automatically invalidate every state regulation in this area. The business of manufacturing and selling contraceptives may be regulated in ways that do not infringe protected individual choices. And even a burdensome regulation may be validated by a sufficiently compelling state interest. In *Roe v. Wade*, for example, after determining that the "right of privacy . . . encompass[es] a woman's decision whether or not to terminate her pregnancy," we cautioned that the right is not absolute, and that certain state interests (in that case, "interests in safeguarding health, in maintaining medical standards, and in protecting potential life") may at some point "become sufficiently compelling to sustain regulation of the factors that govern the abortion decision." "Compelling" is of course the key word; where a decision as fundamental as that whether to bear or beget a child is involved, regulations imposing a burden on it may be justified only by compelling state interests, and must be narrowly drawn to express only those interests. . . .

Restrictions on the Distribution of Contraceptives

We consider first the wider restriction on access to contraceptives created by § 6811(8)'s prohibition of the distribution of nonmedical contraceptives to adults except through licensed pharmacists.

Appellants argue that this Court has not accorded a "right of access to contraceptives" the status of a fundamental aspect of personal liberty. They emphasize that *Griswold v. Connecticut* [1965] struck down a state prohibition of the use of contraceptives, and so had no occasion to discuss laws "regulating their manufacture or sale." *Eisenstadt v. Baird* was decided under the Equal Protection Clause, holding that "whatever the rights of the individual to access to contraceptives may be, the rights must be the same for the unmarried and the married alike." Thus appellants argue that neither case should be treated as reflecting upon the State's power to limit or prohibit distribution of contraceptives to any persons, married or unmarried.

The fatal fallacy in this argument is that it overlooks the underlying premise of those decisions that the Constitution protects

> the right of the individual . . . to be free from unwarranted governmental intrusion into . . . the decision whether to bear or beget a child.

Griswold did state that, by "forbidding the use of contraceptives, rather than regulating their manufacture or sale," the Connecticut statute there had "a maximum destructive impact" on privacy rights. This intrusion into "the sacred precincts of marital bedrooms" made that statute particularly "repulsive." But subsequent decisions have made clear that the constitutional protection of individual autonomy in matters of childbearing is not dependent on that element. *Eisenstadt v. Baird*, holding that the protection is not limited to married couples, characterized the protected right as the "decision whether to bear or beget a child." Similarly, *Roe v. Wade* held that the Constitution protects "a woman's *decision* whether or not to terminate her pregnancy." These decisions put *Griswold* in proper perspective. *Griswold* may no longer be read as holding only that a State may not prohibit a married couple's use of contraceptives. Read in light of its progeny, the teaching of *Griswold* is that the Constitution protects individual decisions in matters of childbearing from unjustified intrusion by the State.

Restrictions on the distribution of contraceptives clearly burden the freedom to make such decisions. A total prohibition against sale of contraceptives, for example, would intrude upon individual decisions in matters of procreation and contraception as harshly as a direct ban on their use. Indeed, in practice, a prohibition against all sales, since more easily and less offensively enforced, might have an even more devastating effect upon the freedom to choose contraception.

The Lack of a Compelling State Interest

An instructive analogy is found in decisions after *Roe v. Wade* that held unconstitutional statutes that did not prohibit abortions outright but limited in a variety of ways a woman's access to them. The significance of these cases is that they establish that the same test must be applied to state regulations that burden an individual's right to decide to prevent conception or terminate pregnancy by substantially limiting access to the means of effectuating that decision as is applied to state statutes that prohibit the decision entirely. Both types of regulation

> may be justified only by a "compelling state interest" ... , and ... must be narrowly drawn to express only the legitimate state interests at stake.

This is so not because there is an independent fundamental "right of access to contraceptives," but because such access is essential to exercise of the constitutionally protected right of decision in matters of childbearing that is the underlying foundation of the holdings in *Griswold, Eisenstadt v. Baird*, and *Roe v. Wade*.

Limiting the distribution of nonprescription contraceptives to licensed pharmacists clearly imposes a significant burden on the right of the individuals to use contraceptives if they choose to do so. . . .

There remains the inquiry whether the provision serves a compelling state interest. Clearly, "interest . . . in maintaining medical standards, and in protecting potential life" [*Roe v. Wade*], cannot be invoked to justify this statute. Insofar as § 6811(8) applies to nonhazardous contraceptives, it bears no relation to the State's interest in protecting health. Nor is the interest in protecting potential life implicated in state regulation of contraceptives.

Appellants therefore suggest that § 6811(8) furthers other state interests. But none of them is comparable to those the Court has heretofore recognized as compelling. . . .

In Planned Parenthood of Central Missouri v. Danforth *(1976), former Missouri attorney general John Danforth argued that minors should not be able to obtain abortions without parental consent. The US Supreme Court maintained that this restriction violated minors' right to privacy and later used the* Danforth *case to overturn laws restricting teen access to contraception.* © Bill Greenblatt/Getty Images.

The Prohibition on Contraceptives for Minors

The question of the extent of state power to regulate conduct of minors not constitutionally regulable when committed by adults is a vexing one, perhaps not susceptible of precise answer. We have been reluctant to attempt to define "the totality of the relationship of the juvenile and the state" [*In re Gault* (1967)]. Certain principles, however, have been recognized. "Minors, as well as adults, are protected by the Constitution, and possess constitutional rights" [*Planned Parenthood of Central Missouri v. Danforth* (1976)]. "[W]hatever may be their precise impact, neither the Fourteenth Amendment nor the Bill of Rights is for adults alone" [*In re Gault*]. On the other hand, we have held in a variety of contexts that "the power of the state to control the conduct of children reaches beyond the scope of its authority over adults" [*Prince v. Massachusetts* (1944)].

Of particular significance to the decision of this case, the right to privacy in connection with decisions affecting procreation extends to minors, as well as to adults. *Planned Parenthood of Central Missouri v. Danforth* held that a State

> may not impose a blanket provision . . . requiring the consent of a parent or person *in loco parentis* [in the place of a parent] as a condition for abortion of an unmarried minor during the first 12 weeks of her pregnancy.

As in the case of the spousal consent requirement struck down in the same case, "the State does not have the constitutional authority to give a third party an absolute, and possibly arbitrary, veto," "'which the state itself is absolutely and totally prohibited from exercising.'" State restrictions inhibiting privacy rights of minors are valid only if they serve "any significant state interest . . . that is not present in the case of an adult." *Planned Parenthood* found that no such interest justified a state requirement of parental consent.

Since the State may not impose a blanket prohibition, or even a blanket requirement of parental consent, on the choice of a minor to terminate her pregnancy, the constitutionality of a blanket prohibition of the distribution of contraceptives to minors is *a fortiori* [for a still stronger reason] foreclosed. The State's interests in protection of the mental and physical health of the pregnant minor, and in protection of potential life are clearly more implicated by the abortion decision than by the decision to use a nonhazardous contraceptive.

The State's Justification for Restricting Minors' Access to Contraceptives

Appellants argue, however, that significant state interests are served by restricting minors' access to contraceptives, because free availability to minors of contraceptives would lead to increased sexual activity among the young, in violation of the policy of New York to discourage such behavior. The argument is that minors' sexual activity may be deterred by increasing the hazards attendant on it. The same argument, however, would support a ban on abortions for minors, or indeed support a prohibition on abortions, or access to contraceptives, for the unmarried, whose sexual activity is also against the public policy of many States. Yet, in each of these areas, the Court has rejected the argument, noting in *Roe v. Wade* that "no court or commentator has taken the argument seriously." The reason for this unanimous rejection was stated in *Eisenstadt v. Baird*:

> It would be plainly unreasonable to assume that [the State] has prescribed pregnancy and the birth of an unwanted child [or the physical and psychological dangers of an abortion] as punishment for fornication.

We remain reluctant to attribute any such "scheme of values" to the State.

Moreover, there is substantial reason for doubt whether limiting access to contraceptives will, in fact, substantially discour-

TEEN CONTRACEPTIVE USE

The rate of contraception use among teens during their first sexual experience is increasing.

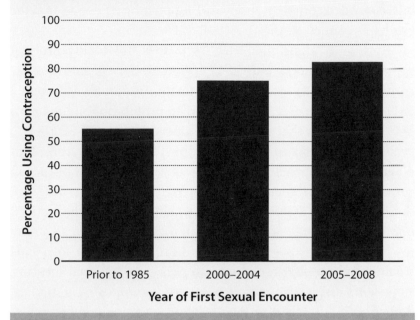

Year of First Sexual Encounter

Taken from: Guttmacher Institute, "Facts on American Teens' Sexual and Reproductive Health," February 2012.

age early sexual behavior. Appellants themselves conceded in the District Court that "there is no evidence that teenage extramarital sexual activity increases in proportion to the availability of contraceptives," and accordingly offered none, in the District Court or here. Appellees, on the other hand, cite a considerable body of evidence and opinion indicating that there is no such deterrent effect. Although we take judicial notice, as did the District Court, that with or without access to contraceptives, the incidence of sexual activity among minors is high, and the consequence of such activity are frequently devastating, the studies cited by appellees play no part in our decision. It is enough that we again confirm the principle that, when a State, as here, burdens the exercise of a fundamental right, its attempt to justify that burden as a rational means for the accomplishment of some significant state policy requires more than a bare assertion, based on a conceded complete absence of supporting evidence, that the burden is connected to such a policy.

Appellants argue that New York does not totally prohibit distribution of contraceptives to minors under 16, and that, accordingly, § 611(8) cannot be held unconstitutional. Although § 6811(8), on its face, is a flat unqualified prohibition, Educ.Law § 6807(b) provides that nothing in Education Law §§ 6800-6826 shall be construed to prevent "[a]ny physician . . . from supplying his patients with such drugs as [he] . . . deems proper in connection with his practice." This narrow exception, however, does not save the statute. As we have held above as to limitations upon distribution to adults, less than total restrictions on access to contraceptives that significantly burden the right to decide whether to bear children must also pass constitutional scrutiny. Appellants assert no medical necessity for imposing a medical limitation on the distribution of nonprescription contraceptives to minors. Rather, they argue that such a restriction serves to emphasize to young people the seriousness with which the State views the decision to engage in sexual intercourse at an early age. But this is only another form of the argument that juvenile sexual conduct will be deterred by making contraceptives more difficult to obtain. Moreover, that argument is particularly poorly suited to the restriction appellants are attempting to justify, which on appellants' construction delegates the State's authority to disapprove of minors' sexual behavior to physicians, who may exercise it arbitrarily, either to deny contraceptives to young people, or to undermine the State's policy of discouraging illicit early sexual behavior. This the State may not do.

> *"If the State decides to require a pregnant minor to obtain one or both parents' consent to an abortion, it also must provide an alternative procedure."*

States May Require Parental Consent for Abortion if an Alternative Is Available

The Supreme Court's Decision

Lewis F. Powell Jr.

In the following viewpoint, US Supreme Court Justice Lewis F. Powell Jr. argues that states may require parental consent in order for a minor to get an abortion, as long as the state provides an alternative procedure for the minor to obtain permission. Powell maintains that the court's previous decisions support the unique treatment of minors under the law, including respect for the role of parents. Powell notes that the court determined in Planned Parenthood of Central Missouri v. Danforth *(1976) that the state may not require parental consent with no alternatives, but he concludes that states may require parental consent as long as they allow the possibility for anonymous and quick judicial authorization as well. Powell was an associate justice on the US Supreme Court from 1972 until 1987.*

Lewis F. Powell Jr., Plurality opinion, *Bellotti v. Baird*, US Supreme Court, July 2, 1979.

A child, merely on account of his minority, is not beyond the protection of the Constitution. As the Court said in *In re Gault* (1967), "whatever may be their precise impact, neither the Fourteenth Amendment nor the Bill of Rights is for adults alone." This observation, of course, is but the beginning of the analysis. The Court long has recognized that the status of minors under the law is unique in many respects. As Mr. Justice [Felix] Frankfurter aptly put it: "Children have a very special place in life which law should reflect. Legal theories and their phrasing in other cases readily lead to fallacious reasoning if uncritically transferred to determination of a State's duty towards children" [*May v. Anderson* (1953) (concurring opinion)]. The unique role in our society of the family, the institution by which "we inculcate and pass down many of our most cherished values, moral and cultural" [*Moore v. East Cleveland* (1977) (plurality opinion)], requires that constitutional principles be applied with sensitivity and flexibility to the special needs of parents and children. We have recognized three reasons justifying the conclusion that the constitutional rights of children cannot be equated with those of adults: the peculiar vulnerability of children; their inability to make critical decisions in an informed, mature manner; and the importance of the parental role in child rearing.

The Vulnerability of Children

The Court's concern for the vulnerability of children is demonstrated in its decisions dealing with minors' claims to constitutional protection against deprivations of liberty or property interests by the State. With respect to many of these claims, we have concluded that the child's right is virtually coextensive with that of an adult. For example, the Court has held that the Fourteenth Amendment's guarantee against the deprivation of liberty without due process of law is applicable to children in juvenile delinquency proceedings. In particular, minors involved in such proceedings are entitled to adequate notice, the assistance of counsel, and the opportunity to confront their accusers.

They can be found guilty only upon proof beyond a reasonable doubt, and they may assert the privilege against compulsory self-incrimination. Similarly, in *Goss v. Lopez* (1975), the Court held that children may not be deprived of certain property interests without due process.

These rulings have not been made on the uncritical assumption that the constitutional rights of children are indistinguishable from those of adults. Indeed, our acceptance of juvenile courts distinct from the adult criminal justice system assumes that juvenile offenders constitutionally may be treated differently from adults. In order to preserve this separate avenue for dealing with minors, the Court has said that hearings in juvenile delinquency cases need not necessarily "conform with all of the requirements of a criminal trial or even of the usual administrative hearing'" [*In re Gault* quoting *Kent v. United States* (1966)]. Thus, juveniles are not constitutionally entitled to trial by jury in delinquency adjudications. Viewed together, our cases show that although children generally are protected by the same constitutional guarantees against governmental deprivations as are adults, the State is entitled to adjust its legal system to account for children's vulnerability and their needs for "concern, . . . sympathy, and . . . paternal attention."

The Immaturity of Children

Second, the Court has held that the States validly may limit the freedom of children to choose for themselves in the making of important, affirmative choices with potentially serious consequences. These rulings have been grounded in the recognition that, during the formative years of childhood and adolescence, minors often lack the experience, perspective, and judgment to recognize and avoid choices that could be detrimental to them.

Ginsberg v. New York (1968), illustrates well the Court's concern over the inability of children to make mature choices, as the First Amendment rights involved are clear examples of constitutionally protected freedoms of choice. At issue was a criminal

STATE LAWS ON PARENTAL INVOLVEMENT IN MINORS' ABORTIONS

State	Parental Involvement			Judicial Bypass Available
	Consent Only	Notification and Consent	Notification Only	
Alabama	X	---	---	X
Alaska	---	---	X	X
Arizona	X✪	---	---	X
Arkansas	X✪	---	---	X✪
California	▼	---	---	---
Colorado	---	---	X	X
Delaware◊	---	---	X+◊	X
Florida	---	---	X	X
Georgia	---	---	X	X
Idaho	X	---	---	X
Illinois	---	---	△	△
Indiana	X	---	---	X
Iowa	---	---	X	X
Kansas	Both parents✪	---	---	X
Kentucky	X	---	---	X
Louisiana	X✪	---	---	X
Maryland	---	---	X+	---
Massachusetts	X	---	---	X
Michigan	X	---	---	X
Minnesota	---	---	Both parents	X
Mississippi	Both parents	---	---	X
Missouri	X	---	---	X
Montana◊	---	---	X	X
Nebraska	X✪	---	---	X
Nevada	---	---	▼	---

Taken from: Guttmacher Institute, "Parental Involvement in Minors' Abortions," *State Policies in Brief*, April 1, 2013.

STATE LAWS ON PARENTAL INVOLVEMENT IN MINORS' ABORTIONS (continued)

State	Parental Involvement			Judicial Bypass Available
	Consent Only	Notification and Consent	Notification Only	
New Hampshire	---	---	X	X
New Jersey	---	---	▼	---
New Mexico	▼	---	---	---
North Carolina	X	---	---	X
North Dakota	Both parents	---	---	X
Ohio	X	---	---	X
Oklahoma	---	X	---	X
Pennsylvania	X	---	---	X
Rhode Island	X	---	---	X
South Carolina ◇	x✛	---	---	x◇
South Dakota	---	---	X	X
Tennessee	X	---	---	X
Texas	---	x✪	---	X
Utah	---	X	---	x★
Virginia	---	x✪	---	X
West Virginia	---	---	x✛	x✪
Wisconsin	x✛	---	---	x✪
Wyoming	---	X	---	X

▼   *Enforcement permanently enjoined by court order; policy not in effect.*

△   *Enforcement temporarily enjoined by court order; policy not in effect.*

✪   *Requires parental consent documentation to be notarized.*

✛   *Allows specific health professionals to waive parental involvement in limited circumstances.*

◇   *While most state laws apply to minors, the laws in Delaware and Montana apply to women younger than sixteen, and South Carolina's law applies to those younger than seventeen.*

★   *The provision applies only to parental consent requirements.*

Taken from: Guttmacher Institute, "Parental Involvement in Minors' Abortions," *State Policies in Brief*, April 1, 2013.

conviction for selling sexually oriented magazines to a minor under the age of 17 in violation of a New York state law. It was conceded that the conviction could not have stood under the First Amendment if based upon a sale of the same material to an adult. Notwithstanding the importance the Court always has attached to First Amendment rights, it concluded that "even where there is an invasion of protected freedoms 'the power of the state to control the conduct of children reaches beyond the scope of its authority over adults . . .'," [quoting *Prince v. Massachusetts* (1944)]. The Court was convinced that the New York Legislature rationally could conclude that the sale to children of the magazines in question presented a danger against which they should be guarded. It therefore rejected the argument that the New York law violated the constitutional rights of minors.

The Importance of Parental Authority

Third, the guiding role of parents in the upbringing of their children justifies limitations on the freedoms of minors. The State commonly protects its youth from adverse governmental action and from their own immaturity by requiring parental consent to or involvement in important decisions by minors. But an additional and more important justification for state deference to parental control over children is that "[t]he child is not the mere creature of the State; those who nurture him and direct his destiny have the right, coupled with the high duty, to recognize and prepare him for additional obligations" [*Pierce v. Society of Sisters* (1925)]. "The duty to prepare the child for 'additional obligations' . . . must be read to include the inculcation of moral standards, religious beliefs, and elements of good citizenship" [*Wisconsin v. Yoder* (1972)]. This affirmative process of teaching, guiding, and inspiring by precept and example is essential to the growth of young people into mature, socially responsible citizens.

We have believed in this country that this process, in large part, is beyond the competence of impersonal political institutions. Indeed, affirmative sponsorship of particular ethical, religious, or political beliefs is something we expect the State not to attempt in a society constitutionally committed to the ideal of individual liberty and freedom of choice. Thus, "[i]t is cardinal with us that the custody, care and nurture of the child reside first in the parents, whose primary function and freedom include preparation for obligations the state can neither supply nor hinder" [*Prince v. Massachusetts*].

Unquestionably, there are many competing theories about the most effective way for parents to fulfill their central role in assisting their children on the way to responsible adulthood. While we do not pretend any special wisdom on this subject, we cannot ignore that central to many of these theories, and deeply rooted in our Nation's history and tradition, is the belief that the parental role implies a substantial measure of authority over one's children. Indeed, "constitutional interpretation has consistently recognized that the parents' claim to authority in their own household to direct the rearing of their children is basic in the structure of our society" [*Ginsberg v. New York*].

Properly understood, then, the tradition of parental authority is not inconsistent with our tradition of individual liberty; rather, the former is one of the basic presuppositions of the latter. Legal restrictions on minors, especially those supportive of the parental role, may be important to the child's chances for the full growth and maturity that make eventual participation in a free society meaningful and rewarding. Under the Constitution, the State can "properly conclude that parents and others, teachers for example, who have [the] primary responsibility for children's well-being are entitled to the support of laws designed to aid discharge of that responsibility.". . .

The Requirement of Parental Consultation

As immature minors often lack the ability to make fully informed choices that take account of both immediate and long-range consequences, a State reasonably may determine that parental consultation often is desirable and in the best interest of the minor. It may further determine, as a general proposition, that such consultation is particularly desirable with respect to the abortion decision—one that for some people raises profound moral and religious concerns. As Mr. Justice [Potter] Stewart wrote in concurrence in *Planned Parenthood of Central Missouri v. Danforth* [1976]:

> There can be little doubt that the State furthers a constitutionally permissible end by encouraging an unmarried pregnant minor to seek the help and advice of her parents in making the very important decision whether or not to bear a child. That is a grave decision, and a girl of tender years, under emotional stress, may be ill-equipped to make it without mature advice and emotional support. It seems unlikely that she will obtain adequate counsel and support from the attending physician at an abortion clinic, where abortions for pregnant minors frequently take place.

But we are concerned here with a constitutional right to seek an abortion. The abortion decision differs in important ways from other decisions that may be made during minority. The need to preserve the constitutional right and the unique nature of the abortion decision, especially when made by a minor, require a State to act with particular sensitivity when it legislates to foster parental involvement in this matter.

A Minor's Abortion Decision

The pregnant minor's options are much different from those facing a minor in other situations, such as deciding whether to marry. A minor not permitted to marry before the age of majority is required simply to postpone her decision. She and her intended spouse may preserve the opportunity for later marriage should they continue to desire it. A pregnant adolescent, however, cannot preserve for long the possibility of aborting, which effectively expires in a matter of weeks from the onset of pregnancy.

William and Karen Bell became activists against parental consent laws after the death of their daughter Becky, who they believe died from a self-induced abortion. In Bellotti v. Baird *(1979), the US Supreme Court ruled that states with parental consent laws must provide teens with alternative ways to obtain permission for an abortion.* © Michael L. Abramson/Time & Life Pictures/Getty Images.

Moreover, the potentially severe detriment facing a pregnant woman is not mitigated by her minority. Indeed, considering her probable education, employment skills, financial resources, and emotional maturity, unwanted motherhood may be exceptionally burdensome for a minor. In addition, the fact of having a child brings with it adult legal responsibility, for parenthood, like attainment of the age of majority, is one of the traditional criteria for the termination of the legal disabilities of minority. In sum, there are few situations in which denying a minor the right to make an important decision will have consequences so grave and indelible.

Yet, an abortion may not be the best choice for the minor. The circumstances in which this issue arises will vary widely. In a given case, alternatives to abortion, such as marriage to the father of the child, arranging for its adoption, or assuming the responsibilities of motherhood with the assured support of family, may be feasible and relevant to the minor's best interests. Nonetheless, the abortion decision is one that simply cannot be postponed, or it will be made by default with far-reaching consequences.

For these reasons, as we held in *Planned Parenthood of Central Missouri v. Danforth*, "the State may not impose a blanket provision . . . requiring the consent of a parent or person in loco parentis [in place of a parent] as a condition for abortion of an unmarried minor during the first 12 weeks of her pregnancy." Although, such deference to parents may be permissible with respect to other choices facing a minor, the unique nature and consequences of the abortion decision make it inappropriate "to give a third party an absolute, and possibly arbitrary, veto over the decision of the physician and his patient to terminate the patient's pregnancy, regardless of the reason for withholding the consent." We therefore conclude that if the State decides to require a pregnant minor to obtain one or both parents' consent to an abortion, it also must provide an alternative procedure whereby authorization for the abortion can be obtained.

A pregnant minor is entitled in such a proceeding to show either: (1) that she is mature enough and well enough informed to make her abortion decision, in consultation with her physician, independently of her parents' wishes; (2) that even if she is not able to make this decision independently, the desired abortion would be in her best interests. The proceeding in which this showing is made must assure that a resolution of the issue, and any appeals that may follow, will be completed with anonymity and sufficient expedition to provide an effective opportunity for an abortion to be obtained. In sum, the procedure must ensure that the provision requiring parental consent does not in fact amount to the "absolute, and possibly arbitrary, veto" that was found impermissible in *Danforth*.

> *"Parental consent laws boast a
> 71 percent nationwide approval rating,
> protect the health and well-being of
> minors, respect parental rights, and
> save the lives of unborn babies."*

Parental Involvement Laws for Abortion Protect Minors and Parents

Mary E. Harned

In the following viewpoint, Mary E. Harned argues that parental involvement laws for abortion protect minors and parents. Harned contends that current parental notification laws could benefit from better enforcement and more stringent requirements. She argues that clarification is needed for courts in assessing a minor's maturity level, should a minor use the courts to attempt to bypass the parental involvement requirement. Harned is staff counsel for Americans United for Life, a nonprofit law and policy organization that works to protect life under the law.

In 2011, Connecticut—one of only 12 states without a law requiring parental consent or notification before a minor may obtain an abortion—drew national attention when legislative consideration of a bill that would require parental consent for the use of tanning parlors evolved into an abortion debate. One brave legislator confronted his colleagues with a disturbing fact: while the state requires parental consent for tattooing and body piercing, and intended to extend that requirement to the use of tanning parlors, minors may obtain an abortion in Connecticut without any parental involvement. However, when the state senator tried to add a provision requiring parental consent for abortion to the bill, the legislature abandoned it altogether.

Parental Involvement Laws Benefit Teens

It is difficult to comprehend the Connecticut legislature's strong opposition to a law requiring parental consent prior to a minor's abortion, when parental consent laws boast a 71 percent nationwide approval rating, protect the health and well-being of minors, respect parental rights, and save the lives of unborn babies. In fact, this popular legislation saw a rebirth in 2011, with at least 24 states considering one or more measures to enact new or strengthen existing consent or notification requirements.

Why the interest in and support for these laws? The medical, emotional, and psychological consequences of abortion are often serious and can be lasting, particularly when the patient is immature. Moreover, parents usually possess information essential to a physician's exercise of his or her best medical judgment concerning the minor. Parents who are aware that their daughter has had an abortion may better ensure the best post-abortion medical attention. Further, minors who obtain "secret" abortions often do so at the behest of the older men who impregnated them, and then return to abusive situations. News stories frequently reveal yet another teen that has been sexually abused by a person in authority—a coach, teacher, or other authority figure. Every day, teens are taken to abortion clinics without the consent or even the knowledge of their parents. Minors are at risk in every state in which parental involvement laws have not been enacted or are easily circumvented.

In addition, parental involvement laws save the lives of unborn babies by reducing the demand for abortions by minors. For example, a 1996 study revealed that "parental involvement laws appear to decrease minors' demands for abortion by 13 to 25 percent." A 2008 study showed that parental consent laws reduce the minor abortion rate by 18.7 percent. With the loving support of their parents, many young women are able to bring their babies into the world and not face the physical risks and emotional devastation that abortions can bring.

The Constitutionality of Parental Involvement Laws

The U.S. Supreme Court has reviewed statutes requiring parental consent or notification before a minor may obtain an abortion on 11 different occasions. The Court's decisions in these cases provide state legislators with concrete guidelines on how to draft parental involvement laws that will be upheld by the courts.

Based upon Supreme Court precedent and subsequent lower federal court decisions, a parental involvement law is constitutional and does not place an undue burden on minors if it contains the following provisions:

For consent, no physician may perform an abortion upon a minor or incompetent person unless the physician has the consent of one parent or legal guardian. For notice, no physician may perform an abortion upon a minor or incompetent person unless the physician performing the abortion has given 48 hours notice to a parent or legal guardian of the minor or incompetent person.

An exception to the consent or notice requirement exists when there is a medical emergency or when notice is waived by the person entitled to receive the notice.

A minor may bypass the requirement through the courts (i.e., judicial waiver or bypass).

Many states require minors to obtain parental consent for an abortion. Some argue that parental involvement laws keep teen girls safe and protect the rights of parents. © Jim Craigmyle/Corbis.

AUL [Americans United for Life] has drafted both a model "Parental Consent for Abortion Act" as well as a "Parental Notification of Abortion Act," which are based upon Supreme Court precedent and take these issues into consideration.

The Judicial Bypass Requirement

In *Bellotti v. Baird (Bellotti II)* [1979], the Court held that a state which requires a pregnant minor to obtain one or both parents' consent to an abortion must "provide an alternative procedure whereby authorization for the abortion can be obtained." This procedure must include the following four elements:

- An allowance for the minor to show that "she is mature enough and well enough informed to make her abortion decision, in consultation with her physician, independently of her parents' wishes;"

- An allowance for the minor to alternatively show that "even if she is not able to make this decision independently, the desired abortion would be in her best interests;"

- The proceedings in which one of these showings is made must be "completed with anonymity;" and
- The proceedings in which one of these showings is made must be "completed with . . . sufficient expedition to provide an effective opportunity for an abortion to be obtained."

In *Ohio v. Akron Center for Reproductive Health (Akron II)* [1990], the Court left open the question of whether a statute requiring parental notice rather than consent required bypass procedures. The Court stated that given "the greater intrusiveness of consent statutes . . . a bypass procedure that will suffice for a consent statute will suffice also for a notice statute." In other words, when a state includes in its parental notification law bypass procedures that meet the constitutional requirements for a consent bypass, the state's bypass procedures are unquestionably constitutional.

The Medical Emergency Exception

In the 1992 case *Planned Parenthood v. Casey*, a plurality of the United States Supreme Court reaffirmed that a state may constitutionally "require a minor seeking an abortion to obtain the consent of a parent or guardian, provided that there is an adequate judicial bypass procedure." The Court further held that an exception to the parental consent requirement for a "medical emergency" was sufficient to protect a minor's health, and imposed "no undue burden" on her access to abortion.

The Supreme Court noted that the Court of Appeals construed the phrase "serious risk" in the definition of "medical emergency" to include serious conditions that would affect the health of the minor. The lower court stated, "We read the medical emergency exception as intended by the Pennsylvania legislature to assure that compliance with its abortion regulations would not in any way pose a significant threat to the life or health of a woman." Based on this reading, the Court in *Casey* held that the medical emergency definition "imposes no undue burden on a woman's abortion right."

The Need for Parental Involvement Law Enhancements

Tragically, it is often easy for abortion providers to sidestep a law requiring parental consent or notice by claiming they were "duped" into accepting consent from or providing notice to individuals fraudulently representing themselves as the parents or guardians of minors. Other potential loopholes in parental consent or notice statutes include: the inappropriate use of an emergency exception by an abortion provider; exploitation of the judicial bypass system through "forum shopping" (finding courts likely to grant a judicial bypass); a low burden of proof for a minor to show that she is mature enough to make her own abortion decision, or that parental consent or notice is not in her best interest; and a lack of guidance to courts on how to evaluate a minor's maturity or what is in her best interest.

To assist states in better protecting minors and parental rights, AUL has drafted the "Parental Involvement Enhancement Act" to reinforce existing parental involvement laws with the enhancements discussed below.

In parental consent states, a consenting parent or guardian should be required to present government-issued identification before a minor obtains an abortion. In parental notice states, a parent or guardian should be required to present identification when waiving the right to notice. In addition to providing identification, a parent or guardian should provide documentation proving that they are the parent or legal guardian of the minor seeking an abortion. Copies of the identification and proof of relationship must then be kept by the abortion clinic in the minor's medical records. When such actions are required, ignorance of an adult's true identity is not an excuse for failing to follow the law.

Another method states may utilize to ensure that the appropriate person is providing consent or waiving notice is to require the notarization of the applicable form(s). Like the identification and proof of relationship requirements discussed above, notari-

PUBLIC OPINION ON PARENTAL CONSENT

Do you favor or oppose a law requiring women under eighteen to get parental consent for an abortion?

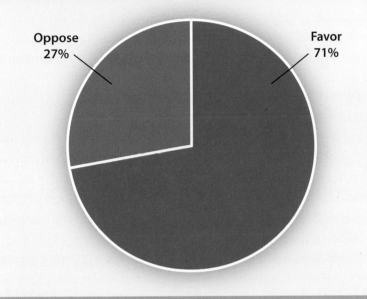

Oppose
27%

Favor
71%

Taken from: Gallup, "US Support for Specific Abortion Restrictions," July 15–17, 2011.

zation requirements help ensure that the correct person has consented or has been notified of plans to perform an abortion on a minor. Further, it is difficult for abortion providers to subvert this requirement.

A "medical emergency" exception in parental involvement laws should not be a license for abortion providers to circumvent the law. Further, a minor who has an abortion following a medical emergency will often require more follow-up care and support from her parents or guardians. Therefore, states can ensure that parental involvement laws are not circumvented and that minors are better protected by requiring abortion providers to promptly notify a parent or guardian that a minor had an "emergency" abortion, the reason for the abortion, and a description of necessary follow-up care.

Some judges or courts are more inclined to grant judicial waiver requests than others. Undoubtedly, abortion providers know which judges or courts are "friendly" to subverting parental rights, and may guide minors to seek a bypass in those courts. To prevent this and better protect minors, states may require a minor to seek a bypass in a court of jurisdiction within her home county.

The Need to Enhance Judicial Bypass Requirements

States may require courts to find "clear and convincing evidence"—evidence showing a high probability of truth of the factual matter at issue—that a minor is either: 1) sufficiently mature and well-informed to consent to an abortion without parental involvement; or 2) that an abortion without parental involvement is in her best interest. "Clear and convincing evidence" is an intermediate standard of proof—higher than "preponderance of the evidence" (more likely than not), but lower than "beyond a reasonable doubt" (used in criminal cases). While judges have broad discretion under most parental involvement laws (their decision to grant a bypass is not subject to review), the "clear and convincing evidence" standard better ensures that judges carefully examine and weigh the facts presented to them in bypass proceedings.

Courts benefit from the provision of specific standards for judicial review in evaluating judicial bypass petitions. Currently, most consent and notice requirements contain very basic criteria, simply requiring that the minor be mature enough to make the decision, or requiring that the abortion be in the minor's "best interest."

An Arizona appellate court case [*In the Matter of B.S.* (Ariz. Ct. App. 2003)] delineated criteria that a judge should use in evaluating the maturity of a minor petitioning for judicial bypass. Specifically, the court's decision:

- Endorsed an examination of the minor's "experience, perspective, and judgment"; Defined "experience" as "all that has happened to the minor in her lifetime including things she has seen or done;"
- Provided that, in assessing a minor's experience level, the court should consider such things as the minor's age and experiences working outside the home, living away from home, handling personal finances, and making other "significant decisions;"
- Defined "perspective," in the context of an abortion decision as the "minor's ability to appreciate and understand the relative gravity and possible detrimental impact of available options, as well as the potential consequences of each;"
- Recommended that, in assessing a minor's perspective on her abortion decision, the court should examine the steps she took to explore her options and the extent to which she considered and weighed the potential consequences of each option;
- Defined "judgment" as the "minor's intellectual and emotional ability to make the abortion decision without the [involvement] of her parents or guardians;"
- Provided that, in assessing judgment, the court should examine the minor's conduct since learning of her pregnancy and her intellectual ability to understand her options and make an informed decision.

This decision provides an excellent example of how, based upon Supreme Court precedent, the more basic judicial bypass requirements can be enhanced.

To further assist courts with their evaluation, states may permit a court to refer a minor for a mental health evaluation. This type of measure protects minors from their own immaturity or from coercion or abuse by others.

> "Forced parental involvement in teens'
> contraceptive decisions endangers teens'
> health and violates their constitutional
> rights."

Obstacles to Abortion, Contraception, and Sex Education Endanger Teens

Center for Reproductive Rights

In the following viewpoint, the Center for Reproductive Rights argues that state laws and policies in the United States regarding reproductive health services are endangering the health of teenagers and violating the rights of young women. The author contends that barriers on teens' access to confidential health services endanger their health, and parental involvement requirements violate their constitutional rights. The Center for Reproductive Rights claims that teenagers have the right to comprehensive sexuality education and confidential health care. The Center for Reproductive Rights is an international reproductive rights organization that uses the law to advance reproductive freedom as a fundamental human right.

Young women face particular obstacles to accessing reproductive health services and information. In addition to laws requiring parental involvement before a minor can obtain an abortion, they may face state laws and policies that: (a) threaten their confidentiality when seeking any reproductive health services; (b) hinder their access to contraception, or (c) deny them age-appropriate sexuality education at school. The Center [for Reproductive Rights] works to protect adolescents' rights and health by fighting to prevent passage of these laws and policies, and by challenging them in court where possible.

Restricting Confidential Health Services Endangers Teens' Health

Placing barriers on teens' access to confidential health services directly endangers their health and welfare because it deters them from seeking the reproductive and sexual health-care services and information they need to prevent unwanted pregnancies, protect their mental and physical health, and avoid sexually transmissible diseases.

In the last decade, under the guise of trying to protect teens from sexual abuse, several states have attempted to use child abuse and statutory rape reporting laws to prevent teens from accessing confidential reproductive health care services. For example, in 2003, the Kansas Attorney General [A.G.] construed the state's child-abuse reporting law to require that doctors, school counselors, therapists and other professionals report any sexual activity involving a minor under the age of 16 as evidence of sexual abuse. The law was so broad as to require a psychologist to report a teen who disclosed that she had "made out" with her same-aged boyfriend. The Center brought a lawsuit against the A.G.'s interpretation, and succeeded in getting it blocked by a federal court. In another example, in 2005, the Attorney General of Indiana and state Medicaid investigators attempted to obtain the medical records of teens served by a family planning clinic, allegedly to investigate accusations that the clinic had failed to properly report cases of abuse.

The Constitution Protects
Contraception Access and Use

The constitutional right to privacy protects adolescents' access to and use of contraception. Forced parental involvement in teens' contraceptive decisions endangers teens' health and violates their constitutional rights. Research shows that requiring minors to tell a parent before they can access contraception delays or prevents them from seeking reproductive health services, but does not reduce their sexual activity. When teenagers do not seek reproductive health services, they forego not only contraceptive services, but also testing and treatment for sexually transmitted infections, routine gynecological exams, and other vital health care. Consequently, the nation's medical and public health organizations consistently oppose forced parental involvement in minors' efforts to seek contraception. These groups include: the American Academy of Family Physicians, the American Academy of Pediatrics, the American College of Obstetricians and Gynecologists, the American Medical Women's Association, and The Society for Adolescent Health and Medicine.

Nonetheless, over the past three decades, state legislatures have repeatedly attempted to restrict teens' access to reproductive health care by trying to impose parental consent requirements on minors seeking contraception through clinics funded by Title X and Medicaid. However, because Title X and Medicaid protect teens' privacy and explicitly prohibit parental consent requirements for teens seeking contraception, those attempts have thus far been invalidated when challenged in court. Nevertheless, in both 2007 and 2009, federal legislation was introduced in the House that would have required Title X family planning clinics to provide written notice to a parent or legal guardian before providing an adolescent with any form of contraception. Fortunately, those bills did not make it out of the House committee.

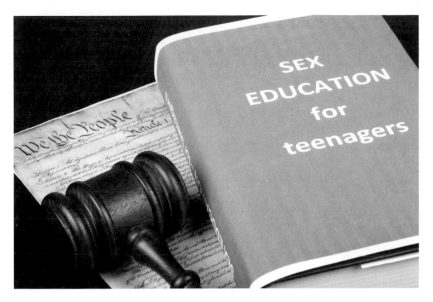

Teen access to contraception, abortion, and comprehensive sex education are contested issues in US society. Some argue that restrictions on teens' access to confidential health services violate their constitutional rights. © ericsphotography/Shutterstock.

The Need for Comprehensive Sexuality Education

Abstinence-only education programs taught in U.S. public schools suffer from numerous flaws, including that they are ineffective in causing teens to remain abstinent; they provide students misinformation and fail to provide information necessary to avoid pregnancy and sexually transmitted infections; they ignore the needs and circumstances of lesbian, gay, bisexual, and transgender youth; they propagate religious values; and they harm the health and well-being of girls by teaching gender stereotypes as "facts."

Since 1982, the federal government has spent over 1.5 billion dollars on grants and matching grants to promote the teaching of abstinence-only-until-marriage education programs. Recipients of much of this funding must comply with guidelines that preclude them from teaching comprehensive sex education. Abstinence-only education teaches that abstinence from sexual

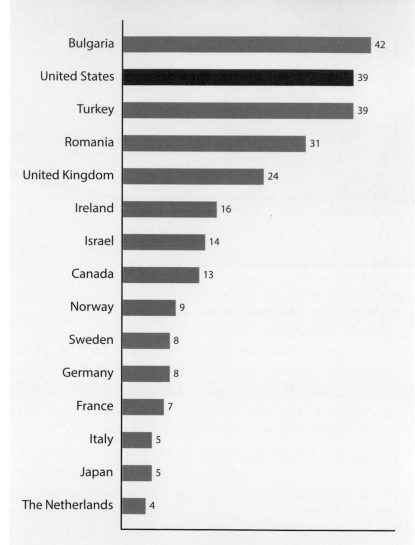

US TEEN BIRTH RATE IS HIGHEST AMONG ALL INDUSTRIALIZED COUNTRIES

Country	
Bulgaria	42
United States	39
Turkey	39
Romania	31
United Kingdom	24
Ireland	16
Israel	14
Canada	13
Norway	9
Sweden	8
Germany	8
France	7
Italy	5
Japan	5
The Netherlands	4

Live births per 1,000 females age 15–19 years

Taken from: Centers for Disease Control and Prevention, "Teen Birth Rates Declined Again in 2009," July 1, 2011. www.cdc.gov.

activity is the only way to avoid pregnancy out-of-wedlock, sexually transmitted infections, and other associated health problems.

By contrast, comprehensive sex education not only presents abstinence as a positive choice, but it also teaches minors how to prevent pregnancy and sexually transmitted infections, should they engage in sexual activity. Comprehensive sexual education programs help to reduce the rates of maternal mortality, abortion, adolescent pregnancies, and HIV/AIDS. The failure to provide students with comprehensive sex education raises serious public health and human rights concerns, especially since the U.S. has one of the highest rates of teen pregnancy in the developed world and because almost half of the 19 million new sexually transmitted infections each year occur among young people ages 15 to 24. The Center therefore advocates that the federal government and the states cease funding and implementing abstinence-only programs and instead provide students with comprehensive sexuality education.

> "Genuine abstinence education is . . .
> crucial to the physical and psycho-
> emotional well-being of the nation's
> youth."

Teens Should Get Abstinence Education, Not Contraception Information

Mary Frances Boyle

In the following viewpoint, Mary Frances Boyle argues that in-creased US spending on programs to provide birth control at clin-ics and comprehensive sex education in schools is not decreas-ing the amount of unsafe sex. Boyle contends that a focus on contraception-based education contradicts what parents want to teach their children, and she claims that research supports the ef-fectiveness of abstinence-centered education. Finally, she claims that teen sexual activity is not good for teens or society, and policy makers should focus on spreading abstinence education. Boyle is a graduate student of theological ethics at St. Louis University and a former graduate fellow of the Heritage Foundation.

I t's that time of year [September 26, 2011, World Contraception Day] again, and the "safe sex" brigade is out in full force to

Advocates for abstinence-only education argue that it is more effective at reducing unsafe sexual behavior among teens than contraception-based education. © Spencer Grant/Getty Images.

educate your sons and daughters about their sexual and reproductive health.

The Promotion of Contraception for Youth

According to a recent study, more young people throughout the world are having unprotected sex and know less about effective contraception. Now contraception enthusiasts are using this as a call for action to increase youths' access to contraception.

The study shows that the number of young people in the U.S. having unsafe sex with new partners increased by 39 percent in the last three years. But, as Heritage [Foundation] research shows, access to birth control is not the problem. In fact, government-funded Title X clinics operate in nearly every county in the U.S., and they provide birth control to over 4 million women each year. In a recent survey, only 1 percent of low-income women who had children out of wedlock reported that lack of access to contraception played a role in the pregnancy.

However, for decades the United States has increased spending on programs to promote contraception among adolescents. Today, the government spends over $610 million annually on programs to promote "safe sex," and the [US President Barack] Obama Administration has put forth a major effort to expose all American children to comprehensive sex education.

Meanwhile, the ratio of funding for contraception-based education to abstinence-centered education is 16 to 1, and the Obama Administration is doing what it can to make this spending disparity even larger.

The Effectiveness of Abstinence Education

Not only does the policy miss the point that lack of contraception isn't the real problem; it also flies in the face of what parents want to teach their children. According to a 2009 report for the Department of Health and Human Services (HHS), 83 percent of parents support their teens receiving the abstinence message in school. Moreover, the survey shows that 70 percent of parents support abstinence until marriage.

And why not? Abstinent youths show better performance in school, have better emotional health, and are less likely to contract STDs [sexually transmitted diseases]. They also decrease their chances of living in poverty by avoiding childbirth outside of marriage.

Abstinence education is proven to be an effective option as well. A 2010 Heritage report analyzed 22 studies of abstinence education. Overall, 17 of the 22 studies reported statistically significant positive results for abstinence education, such as delayed sexual initiation and reduced levels of early sexual activity.

In the same report, policy analyst Christine Kim writes:

> Teen sexual activity is costly, not just for teens, but also for society. Teens who engage in sexual activity risk a host of negative outcomes including STD infection, emotional and

TEEN SEXUAL ACTIVITY IN THE UNITED STATES

Percentage of high school students who have ever had sexual intercourse

Category	Female	Male	Total
Race/Ethnicity			
White	44.5%	44.0%	44.3%
Black	53.6%	66.9%	60.0%
Hispanic	43.9%	53.0%	48.6%
Grade			
9	27.8%	37.8%	32.9%
10	43.0%	44.5%	43.8%
11	51.9%	54.5%	53.2%
12	63.6%	62.6%	63.1%
Total	**45.6%**	**49.2%**	**47.4%**

Taken from: Centers for Disease Control and Prevention, "Youth Risk Behavior Surveillance—United States 2011," *Morbidity and Mortality Weekly Report (MMWR)*, vol. 61, no. 4, June 8, 2012.

psychological harm, lower educational attainment, and out-of-wedlock childbearing. Genuine abstinence education is therefore crucial to the physical and psycho-emotional well-being of the nation's youth.

The Need for Policy Supporting Abstinence Education

Some congressional initiatives are taking this approach. Representative Randy Hultgren (R-IL) introduced the Abstinence Education Reallocation Act of 2011 (H.R. 2874) earlier this month [October 2011 (the bill did not become law)], which would allow HHS to "award grants on a competitive basis to public and private entities to provide qualified sexual risk avoidance education to youth and their parents." The bill seeks to reallocate current funds to more effective strategies.

In addition, the draft fiscal year 2012 Labor, Health and Human Services funding bill released Friday [September 29, 2011] includes funding for abstinence education. The bill targets $20 million toward competitive grants to provide abstinence education.

This renewed focus on abstinence education better reflects the will of the American people, and it would give youth access to better options when it comes to sexual education.

According to FamilyFacts.org, more than half of all U.S. high school students report remaining abstinent, which represents an 18 percent increase since the 1990s. This is good news, and policymakers should do more to spread abstinence education. It's healthy, it's effective, and it's what parents want. Most importantly, the message of abstinence promotes bright futures for our youth and all of civil society.

> "Federal sponsorship of abstinence-only
> education impairs the constitutional
> rights minors enjoy with respect to
> their sexual health and procreation
> decisions."

Abstinence-Only Education Violates Minors' Constitutional Rights

Hazel Glenn Beh and Milton Diamond

In the following viewpoint, Hazel Glenn Beh and Milton Diamond argue that federal funding of abstinence-only education violates the rights of minors to have access to accurate information about sex. They contend that the justifications for abstinence-only education are analogous to New York State's justifications for the law at issue in Carey v. Population Services International *(1977), which prevented minors from accessing contraception. In* Carey, *the US Supreme Court rejected New York's justifications by asserting minors' right to privacy with respect to procreation, thereby finding laws restricting access to contraception by minors to be unconstitutional. Beh and Diamond argue that the same reasoning applies to the government's attempt to keep sex-education information from minors, thereby proving abstinence-only education*

Hazel Glenn Beh and Milton Diamond, "The Failure of Abstinence-Only Education: Minors Have a Right to Honest Talk About Sex," *Columbia Journal of Gender and Law,* vol. 15, pp. 12–62, 2006 (footnotes and emphasis omitted; subheadings not in original). Copyright © 2006 by Columbia Journal of Gender and Law. All rights reserved. Reproduced by permission.

to be unconstitutional. Beh is a professor of law at the William S. Richardson School of Law at the University of Hawai'i at Manoa and codirector of the school's Health Law Policy Center. Diamond is director of the Pacific Center for Sex and Society at the University of Hawai'i at Manoa.

The federal government spends over $170 million annually to subsidize states and community organizations that provide abstinence-only sex education to America's youth. This type of sex education is limited to teaching that a monogamous, marital, heterosexual relationship is the "expected standard of human activity" and that sex outside such a relationship will be physically and psychologically harmful. Abstinence-only education also advocates only one method to prevent disease and pregnancy, abstinence, and it offers no information concerning contraception and disease prevention except that all methods other than abstinence fail. As a result of its singular focus, the curricula not only pose significant problems with respect to ensuring minors' sexual health, but also ignore the needs of sexual minority youth altogether. . . .

Not only is abstinence-only education harmful for minors, but it also infringes on their privacy and autonomy interests in sexual health and procreation. The current sex education debate is frequently portrayed as a dispute over what values to indoctrinate in American youth; however, this mischaracterizes the real controversy, which is first and foremost about what *information* minors should have, not what *values* they should be taught. When framed in this manner, the privacy and autonomy interests of minors to make their own decisions about their sexual health and procreation choices are implicated.

Balancing Minors' Rights and Parents' Rights

The issues surrounding adolescent sexuality raise nearly irreconcilable tensions between the adolescent, the parent, and the state, because each holds firmly established competing rights and interests. The constitutional infirmities related to federal funding of abstinence-only programs with overt religious messages have been explored elsewhere. However, religious entanglement issues are hardly the most harmful aspects of abstinence-only education. More detrimental is that these curricula endanger the health of minors and abridge the minors' constitutionally recognized privacy and autonomy interests related to sex. Once the federal government affirmatively provides or funds others to provide education about sexual health to minors, it owes minors a curriculum that will not harm them and that will respect, rather than impair, their constitutional rights. The omissions and deceptions prevalent within these unfounded curricula both prevent minors from making informed choices and expose them to potentially grave dangers.

When considering a minor's rights, parental rights and state interests are necessarily implicated as well; however, when either parents or the state are vested with power to make decisions for minors, they are empowered and obliged to act in the child's best interest. Parents are conferred the primary authority to inculcate moral and cultural values and to control the education of their children. This power, however, has traditionally been limited by co-existing duties to serve the interests of the child, and is grounded in the presumption that a parent's "natural bonds of affection lead parents to act in the best interests of children" [*Parham v. J.R.* (1979)].

The state has competing interests aimed at protecting children and society; state interests in fact serve as a limitation on parental authority. In education, the state's interest has garnered a particular judicial respect, with the Supreme Court noting that "[p]roviding public schools ranks at the very apex of the function of a State" [*Wisconsin v. Yoder* (1972)]. Indeed, state interests in education cannot be underestimated, as the Court has characterized the public education of youth as essential to the nation's collective survival as a democratic society, stating that "[a] democratic society rests, for its continuance, upon the healthy, well-rounded growth of young people into full maturity as citizens, with all that implies" [*Prince v. Massachusetts* (1944)]. Like parental rights and "high duties," the state's role in education is characterized as both a state interest and an obligation to prepare minors for full participation in democratic society. Thus, both the rights of parents and the interests of the state are grounded in the presumption that their decisions are designed to protect and serve the needs of the child.

Children have their own rights that must be protected against the excesses of state or parental authority. However, as the Supreme Court has cautioned, in applying constitutional principles to children's rights, courts must demonstrate "sensitivity and flexibility to the special needs of parents and children" [*Bellotti v. Baird* (1979)]. Indeed, the Court has found that "the constitutional rights of children cannot be equated with those of adults" in light of "the peculiar vulnerability of children; their inability to make critical decisions in an informed, mature manner; and the importance of the parental role in child rearing." However, even when a child lacks a current capacity, a child's right to exercise self-determination in the future deserves protection and must be considered when possible.

A particularly complex balancing of these competing interests and rights has occurred when addressing legal issues surrounding adolescent sexuality. This is because minors enjoy constitutional rights, albeit with some limitations, related to access to and decision making about contraception and abortion, as well as other important health matters. When it comes to the issue of sexuality, the Supreme Court has explained that "the right to privacy in connection with decisions affecting procreation extends to minors as well as adults," and thus "[s]tate restrictions inhibiting privacy rights of minors are valid only if they serve 'any significant state interest . . . that is not present in the case of an adult'" [*Carey v. Population Services International* (1977)]. . . .

Protestors rally against the expansion of abstinence-only education in US public schools. Advocates for comprehensive sex education maintain that abstinence-only education violates the constitutional rights of minors and puts their health at risk. © Jeff Fusco/Getty Images.

Abstinence-Only Education Is Unconstitutional

When one puts the minor's interests first, the prerogative of the government to singularly teach abstinence, even if shorn of Establishment Clause implications, rests on shaky constitutional grounds. These curricula impair the rights mature adolescents possess in matters concerning their own sexuality and exceed the government's right to promote its own message over others. By omitting or distorting information about sex and sexual health, including the efficacy of contraception, the consequences of abortion, and methods of disease acquisition and prevention, including specifically pertinent information for those youth that belong to sexual minorities, it is as though these programs have embarked on a scheme to prevent minors from making informed choices about rights the law has long accorded them. It is here that these programs cross the line of constitutionality.

There are well-established limits to the authority of the government to control adolescent procreative rights generally. As established in *Carey v. Population Services International,* "the right to privacy in connection with decisions affecting procreation extends to minors as well as to adults," and thus laws that impair adolescents' privacy rights are "valid only if they serve 'any significant state interest . . . that is not present in the case of an adult.'" *Carey,* decided over two decades ago, remains illustrative of the scope of a minor's procreative rights. The case considered the validity of a New York law that restricted the distribution of contraceptives to minors less than 16 years of age. New York argued that the law was intended to regulate "the morality of minors" and deter "promiscuous intercourse among the young," but the Court held that the law impermissibly burdened a minor's right to obtain contraception and, most notably, did not rationally serve to accomplish a significant state interest.

The justifications offered by New York in *Carey* for its restrictions on minors' access to contraception are remarkably similar to those which proponents of abstinence-only education offer today for restrictions on providing sex information to adolescents. New York claimed that access to contraception might promote adolescent sexual promiscuity; similarly, proponents of abstinence-only education claim that information about contraception might encourage licentious behavior. The *Carey* Court was astutely dubious of that justification in the absence of any proof:

> [T]here is substantial reason for doubt whether limiting access to contraceptives will in fact substantially discourage early sexual behavior. Appellants themselves conceded . . . that "there is no evidence that teenage extramarital sexual activity increases in proportion to the availability of contraceptives," and accordingly offered none. . . . Appellees, on the other hand, cite a considerable body of evidence and opinion indicating that there is no such deterrent effect. Although we take judicial notice, as did the District Court, that with or without access to

contraceptives, the incidence of sexual activity among minors is high, and the consequences of such activity are frequently devastating, the studies cited by appellees play no part in our decision. It is enough that we again confirm the principle that when a State, as here, burdens the exercise of a fundamental right, its attempt to justify that burden as a rational means for the accomplishment of some significant state policy requires more than a bare assertion, based on a conceded complete absence of supporting evidence, that the burden is connected to such a policy.

Just as New York could not rely on a bare assertion that access to contraception might encourage promiscuity, proponents of abstinence-only [education] should not be able to depend on a vague and unsubstantiated claim that information about sex will encourage sexual activity.

Abstinence-Only Education Harms Minors

New York also argued that, because minors could obtain contraceptives from physicians, the statute did not significantly burden a minor's privacy interests. The Court rejected the assertion, explaining that, even though the statute did not amount to a total prohibition on distribution of contraception to minors, it nevertheless constituted a significant burden on the right to decide whether to bear children. Finding "no medical necessity for imposing a medical limitation on the distribution of non-prescription contraceptives to minors," the court determined the law constituted a significant burden on a minor's right "to decide whether to bear children."

Abstinence-only education impairs a minor's decisional interests just as significantly as New York's contraception ban did in *Carey*. Proponents of abstinence-only education defend the curricula, arguing in part that there are other avenues available for minors to obtain more comprehensive information. However, for some minors, there is no other avenue. In states

US SOCIAL SECURITY ACT: DEFINITION OF ABSTINENCE EDUCATION

A. Having as its exclusive purpose teaching the social, psychological, and health gains to be realized by abstaining from sexual activity

B. Teach abstinence from sexual activity outside marriage as the expected standard for all school-age children

C. Teach that abstinence from sexual activity is the only certain way to avoid out-of-wedlock pregnancy, sexually transmitted diseases, and other associated health problems

D. Teach that a mutually faithful, monogamous relationship in the context of marriage is the expected standard of sexual activity

E. Teach that sexual activity outside the context of marriage is likely to have harmful psychological and physical effects

F. Teach that bearing children out of wedlock is likely to have harmful consequences for the child, the child's parents, and society

G. Teach young people how to reject sexual advances and how alcohol and drug use increases vulnerability to sexual advances

H. Teach the importance of attaining self-sufficiency before engaging in sexual activity

Taken from: Title V, Section 510 (b)(2)(A-H) of the Social Security Act (P.L. 104–193).

that rely exclusively on money from federal abstinence-only education funds to teach sex education, a minor's constitutionally protected privacy interests in obtaining information about procreative choices may be significantly burdened because he or she may lack access to other outlets to obtain information.

However, even if one conceded both that the government has no obligation to fund any sex information and that all minors might obtain information elsewhere, such as through alternative school programs, family, friends, or health care providers, the ability of any minor who undergoes abstinence-only sex education to make informed decisions concerning sex is nonetheless significantly hampered both by what abstinence-only education teaches and what it omits. Since participants are erroneously instructed, for example, that abstinence is the only effective way to prevent disease and conception, and are not taught that contraception and condom use are effective methods of avoiding pregnancy and disease, they are burdened by erroneous instruction. Even where other sources of information are available, these students are unlikely to appreciate that they should and could seek more comprehensive sex instruction from a more reliable source. After all, a young person will very likely view a teacher working under the auspices of a program funded by the federal government as reliable and honest.

Minors Have a Right to Accurate Information

Moreover, as in *Carey*, the state interest in current abstinence-only education policy is not justified as a rational means to accomplish a significant state policy. First, the goal of preparing minors to responsibly assume a proper position in democratic society, which underlies the state's interest in education, is not served by a singular focus on abstinence. Shaping values in education by withholding knowledge and information is antithetical to public education's purpose of preparing youth to make the weighty choices and decisions expected of America's citizenry. This is especially true given that [according to law professor and academic administrator Mark G. Yudof,] "[o]ur social ideal is a democratic education, one that both prepares our young to choose for themselves and teaches them that their freedom to do so hinges on their respect and tolerance of the freedom of others to choose differently."

Second, the purpose of sex education is not merely to prepare adolescents to assume a future role as a sexually responsible adult in a democratic society. Biological and psychological realities dictate that sex education must educate minors to act responsibly now, and so teaching about sex cannot be postponed until adulthood. Sex education, because of its relationship to a minor's present health and reproduction rights, necessarily stands on a different footing than more mundane curricular choices, and for this reason the scale must tip in favor of the minor's right to comprehensive sex education. In matters of sexuality, mature adolescents have the capacity to engage in and make choices concerning sexual activities, and thus possess corresponding autonomy and privacy interests. Because adolescents are sexually mature at the time that sex education is presented to them, the minor's right to information is no less than that of an adult's.

State laws have vested in adolescents the right to make certain decisions regarding their sexual activities, and therefore the right to information logically inures to them. In the medical setting, a corollary of the right to consent is the right to receive adequate information to make an informed choice, which resides with the decision-maker. However, abstinence-only education only teaches minors to say "no," ignoring the concomitant right to knowledgably say "yes." Mature minors who are both physically and legally entitled to make sexual and reproductive decisions have a right to adequate information to make informed choices. Although sex education is conceptually different than medical treatment, it touches upon similarly private concerns related to autonomy. This is a crucial point, as adolescents are an underserved medical population, and thus formal sex education may provide the only forum through which teenagers might receive sexual health information.

Third, there can be no legitimate interest in affirmatively and deliberately misleading, deceiving, or depriving adolescents of health information when doing so might expose them to grave harms. Indeed, no one has offered a justification for delivering misleading, deceptive, and ineffective information about this important life topic. Further, requiring teachers to engage in such negative behavior forces educators to violate the educator's code of ethics. . . .

Federal sponsorship of abstinence-only education impairs the constitutional rights minors enjoy with respect to their sexual health and procreation decisions. Abstinence-only education's singular focus on abstinence, and its distortions concerning the effectiveness of methods of contraception and disease prevention, the risks associated with abortion, and the other consequences of sex misleads minors and compromises their ability and right to make informed health decisions. Indeed, recent studies suggest that abstinence curricula put minors at greater health risk than they would have been had they not taken any sex education course at all. Adolescents who have undergone abstinence-only education and who later engage in coital and non-coital activity, as most will prior to marriage, are ill-prepared to protect themselves: they may not use a condom because they do not know how or because they mistakenly believe that condoms are ineffective, may be unaware of the risks they experience when engaging in non-coital sexual activity as a strategy to remain "abstinent," and may be more vulnerable to adverse consequences of unprotected sex because they have not rehearsed and otherwise prepared for the contingency that they will not always be abstinent. Thus, by teaching abstinence as the only effective method to prevent disease and pregnancy, these curricula necessarily fail those adolescents who will hear, but not completely heed, that message. Therefore, federally funded abstinence-only education impairs a minor's ability to make informed choices and therefore impermissibly burdens his or her privacy and autonomy interests.

> "Schools are giving children the
> morning-after pill without notifying
> their parents, let alone getting their
> express approval."

Schools for Contraception

Rich Lowry

In the following viewpoint, Rich Lowry argues that a program in New York City's public schools that provides students with morning-after contraceptives is outlandish. Lowry claims that by setting up the program as a default opt-in program, parents are not rightfully given the opportunity to be involved in decisions about their children. Furthermore, he claims that the program implicitly supports and enables teenage sexual activity when school should be providing education. Lowry is editor of National Review *and a syndicated columnist.*

New York City's public schools do a poor job educating kids. In fairness, though, that's not their expertise. What they excel at is giving out contraceptives.

If there were international comparisons of contraception access at schools, instead of math and reading scores, Singapore would have to look in envy at the achievements of New York City and wonder: What can we do to catch up? Task forces and commissions would be established to study the runaway success of schools in America's greatest city.

New York's schools are outdoing themselves with their latest pedagogical initiative, the Orwellian-named CATCH program, for Connecting Adolescents to Comprehensive Health. "Comprehensive health," of course, means only one particular kind of health, the equally euphemistic "reproductive health."

The schools are giving children the morning-after pill without notifying their parents, let alone getting their express approval. Think *in loco parentis*—if the parent were the president of NARAL Pro-Choice America.

The schools already provide free condoms. Soon enough, the mere distribution of condoms will seem the hallmark of a bygone, more innocent era, like something from the plot of a *Happy Days* episode.

The program to give out morning-after pills—and other oral and injected contraceptives—is now up and running in 13 schools. It is an extension from last year's start in five schools, when more than 550 students received emergency contraception. Parents have to explicitly choose to "opt out" of the program, which, as any behavioral economist will tell you, strongly tips the balance toward its passive acceptance.

The morning-after pill, or Plan B, is a contraceptive, but it is possible—although disputed—that it acts like an abortifacient as well. Its distribution is another step down the slippery slope toward the provision of abortion in the schools. If that sounds outlandish, just wait. Ten years ago, free morning-after pills with no parental notification would have seemed the stuff of dystopian social-conservative fantasy.

There can be no doubt about the direction that the Big Apple's latitudinarian educrats want to go. According to Greg Pfundstein, of the pro-life Chiaroscuro Foundation, one of the "homework" exercises in a proposed New York City sex-education curriculum that became controversial last year included a visit or a call to a

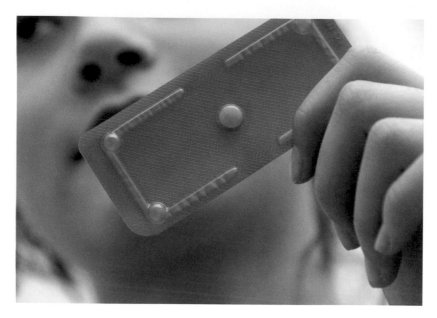

In 2011 New York City's public schools began a program that allows teens to access the morning-after pill. Opponents of the program argue that it promotes teenage sexual activity. © AJPhoto/Photo Researchers, Inc.

"clinic" to find out its hours, what services it provides, and its confidentiality policy.

It can be harder to get an aspirin in some schools around the country than it is now to get Plan B in New York. The schools can give a synthetic female hormone to a girl as young as 14 without so much as a text message to her mom. If the children were given 24-ounce Mountain Dews, Mayor Michael Bloomberg would immediately cashier his schools chancellor. Such is the perverse value system of New York's nanny state that the program ran with no notice to the public—ho-hum—until the *New York Post* broke the story the other day.

Surely, many parents of the kids in the affected schools aren't involved enough in their children's lives. But that doesn't mean schools should keep from them that their daughters are having unprotected sex and might be pregnant.

If easy, widespread access to contraception were the answer to teenage pregnancy, the New York schools would have solved the problem long ago. More access to the latest contraceptive technology isn't going to make a difference. It is true that the schools can't substitute for the discipline and values that kids aren't getting at home. But they shouldn't be the friend and enabler of the sexually active teenager, either.

The schools should do everything they can to create an environment of rigor, with an overwhelming emphasis on future-oriented behavior. Instead, the New York City schools operate on the same mores as a Planned Parenthood clinic does. Parents are a nuisance. No questions are asked. And teenage sex, which is inherently casual sex, is implicitly encouraged.

But don't worry. It will only get worse.

> *"One would think that, after a quarter of a century, the conflict [about contraception and abortion access] would now be over."*

An Educator Recounts His Fight for Privacy in Contraceptive Use

Personal Narrative

Bill Baird

In the following viewpoint, Bill Baird recounts his personal involvement in the struggle to defend the right to privacy as it relates to choices involving contraceptive use and abortion. Baird explains how he was arrested, charged, and sentenced to jail for educating people about birth control and abortion and providing contraception. He recounts his appeal to the US Supreme Court in Eisenstadt v. Baird *(1972), wherein the court ruled in his favor that the right to privacy guaranteed access by unmarried people to contraceptives. He notes that the* Eisenstadt v. Baird *decision was cited several times in* Roe v. Wade *(1973), which upheld the right to privacy with respect to abortion. Baird later went on to fight for the rights of minors to access abortion in* Bellotti v. Baird

(1979). Baird is founder of the Pro-Choice League in Huntington, New York.

Thirty years ago [1967], 679 students at Boston University signed a letter asking me to come to Massachusetts to challenge a nineteenth century law that denied unmarried people access to birth control and abortion devices and information. This law, as amended only the year before, in 1966, declared that the providing or exhibiting of such devices and the printing or dissemination of such information were "Crimes Against Chastity, Morality, Decency, and Good Order," punishable as a felony by up to five years in prison.

The Consequences of Lecturing on Birth Control

These students sought my help because, by this time, I had already been dubbed by the news media a "birth-control crusader." I had opened the nation's first abortion facility in 1964 and twice been imprisoned for teaching birth control and publicly showing birth control devices inside the twenty-five-foot mobile classroom I took to the poor people of Long Island and New Jersey.

So on April 6, 1967, before an overflow audience in excess of 2,000 people, I spoke at Boston University on the public's right to privacy in matters of sexuality, including the right to birth control and abortion. I lectured on birth control methods and devices and emphasized that it is a matter of personal morality and privacy rather than the business of some religious group or government how, when, and with whom one has sexual intercourse. Further, because of its public lobbying stand against birth control and abortion, I stated that the Roman Catholic Church should have its tax-exempt status revoked and be required to register as a foreign lobbyist.

At the end of the lecture I was promptly arrested by members of the vice squad of the Boston police department and charged with two felonies: publicly exhibiting birth control and abortion devices, and giving away a single condom and package of contraceptive foam to a nineteen-year-old, unmarried female student. The event made headlines nationwide.

All of this I had anticipated. What I had not expected, however, was that Planned Parenthood would turn its back on me. In a letter dated June 29, 1967, Hasel Sagoff, executive director of the Massachusetts chapter, clarified to an inquirer the doctrine current at the time. She wrote:

> We are told by our lawyers, experts in constitutional law, that there is no violation of constitutional rights in the present law. They tell us, and we agree, that the only way to liberalize the current law is through the process of filing a bill in the legislature and working for its passage.

Later, Planned Parenthood's national president, Dr. Alan Guttmacher, was quoted by the *Harvard Graduate Bulletin* as saying, "Every couple seeking birth control information should go to a doctor." The *Bulletin* then added, "Planned Parenthood feels it can live with the present law and Baird's efforts are an embarrassment."

Facing Punishment for Distributing Birth Control

I was found guilty of the felony charges by Superior Court Judge Donald Macauley on October 17, 1967—though he stayed the sentence pending the outcome of my appeal to the Massachusetts Supreme Court. That decision came down on May 1, 1968, with the court ruling unanimously that anyone could lecture on birth control and exhibit birth control devices; however, it also ruled four to three that it was still a crime to give any such device to an unmarried individual.

The latter decision led to my sentencing on May 19, 1969, to an unprecedented three months in Boston's Charles Street Jail. The *New York Times* reported:

Bill Baird (right) is a privacy rights activist and founder of the Pro-Choice League. He has been instrumental in the fight for contraception and abortion access. © Larry Morris/The Washington Post/Getty Images.

Before the sentencing, both Judge Macauley and Joseph Balliro, counsel for Mr. Baird, mentioned that they had received more mail on this case than on any other. They said the letters had come from throughout the world and that most had urged leniency for the defendant.

Thirty people, most of them women, peacefully demonstrated on my behalf outside the courthouse.

On February 20, 1970, I began serving my sentence. The experience in the Charles Street Jail was a true nightmare, the details of which I can never forget. Night after night I had to chase rats from the four-by-eight-foot cell in which I was caged, pick bugs from my food, and endure threats of beatings and rape.

The guards repeatedly stripped me naked. On one occasion a fire broke out in the jail, burning an inmate to death.

The US Supreme Court Expands Contraception Access

Meanwhile, my conviction was on appeal to the U.S. Supreme Court. Like 98 percent of all cases they receive, however, the justices initially refused to hear it. Perhaps it was Justice William O. Douglas who encouraged a reappraisal, for he would later write: "The teachings of Baird and those of Galileo might be of a different order; but the suppression of either is equally repugnant."

When the High Court finally heard my case, *Baird v. Eisenstadt*, it looked into the original intent of the Massachusetts law I had broken. The justices found that its actual objective had been to discourage premarital sex and, in the words of the Massachusetts Supreme Court, "to protect purity, to preserve chastity, to encourage continence and self-restraint, to defend the sanctity of the home, and thus to engender in the State and nation a virile and virtuous race of men and women."

So on March 22, 1972—twenty-five years ago—the U.S. Supreme Court ruled six to one in my favor, overturning all similar statutes in twenty-six states which had denied to unmarried people the right to birth control devices and information. Justice William Brennan, writing for the majority, based the decision on the right of privacy. He declared:

> If the right of privacy means anything, it is the right of the individual, married or single, to be free from unwarranted governmental intrusion into matters so fundamentally affecting a person as the decision whether to bear or beget a child.

His word *bear* would prove significant, and I predicted to the press that, because of this decision, all abortion statutes would be repealed within a year's time. And so they were. On January 22, 1973, the Court legalized abortion in *Roe v. Wade*, citing *Baird* six times in its decision.

The Continuing Controversy over Birth Control

One would think that, after a quarter of a century, the conflict would now be over. Yet in 1996, an unmarried seventeen-year-old, Amanda Smisek, was convicted of "fornication" in Idaho in order to teach her "proper morality." Abortion clinics have been bombed, pro-choice Americans have been killed, and the murder of abortion *patients* has been called "justifiable homicide" by anti-abortion activist Father David Trosch.

Fortunately, action continues in support of freedom. Governor Howard Dean, M.D., of Vermont marked the anniversary of *Baird* by naming March 22 as "Right to Privacy Day" in a proclamation which read, "Recognition of the right of privacy has freed millions of men and women from the oppression of unwilling parenthood. . . . This right of privacy is in increasing jeopardy by those who seek to limit its expression." The governors of Massachusetts and Missouri have also recognized this date. The move is on in this twenty-fifth anniversary year to encourage the governors of every state, as well as President [Bill] Clinton, to commemorate this vital liberty by proclaiming March 22 as an annual National Right to Privacy Day.

And now, after a long hiatus, I have been able to return my mobile classroom to the streets of our cities to provide information on birth control and abortion, as well as AIDS prevention, to those Americans who—because of a still deficient sex education and insufficient media advertising devoted to birth control—might secure the information in no other way.

| *"The commonplace belief that the debate over contraception was settled is now unsettled."*

The Fight for Access to Birth Control Continues Today

Jonathan D. Moreno and Frances Kissling

In the following viewpoint, Jonathan D. Moreno and Frances Kissling argue that controversy regarding the birth-control mandate within the Patient Protection and Affordable Care Act of 2010, or ObamaCare, illustrates that opposition to contraception in the United States is still rampant. The authors claim that although the US Supreme Court settled the issue long ago, a resurgence of opposition to sexual liberty threatens to turn back progress on the issue of contraception for the unmarried. Moreno is the David and Lyn Silfen University Professor at the University of Pennsylvania, a senior fellow at the Center for American Progress, and the author of The Body Politic: The Battle Over Science in America. *Kissling is president of the Center for Health, Ethics, and Social Policy and former president of Catholics for Choice.*

While efforts to overturn *Roe v. Wade* [1973] or chip away at abortion access are frequently covered in the media, a longstanding, under-the-radar effort of a number of social and religious conservatives to limit access to contraception has escaped notice—until now. In fact, until recently, any mention of these efforts has been taken as a sign of paranoia or Catholic bashing. Contraception, used by 99 percent of women at some time in their reproductive lives and approved of by just about everyone except the Catholic bishops and the most extreme social conservatives, has for 40 years been considered a settled issue. The FDA [US Food and Drug Administration] approved the birth control pill in 1960 and in 1965 the Supreme Court affirmed the right to use contraception in *Griswold v. Connecticut*.

Contraception Access Spurs Debate

The healthcare reform process has inadvertently undermined that comfortable assumption. The US Conference of Catholic Bishops, the Republican Party and [conservative talk-show host] Rush Limbaugh have all claimed that the inclusion of contraception among a long list of preventive services that employers must insure without cost or co-payments by employees violates religious freedom. For a few weeks it seemed America's pundits and even some liberal Catholics, like [journalist and political commentator] E.J. Dionne, bought the argument. A deft accommodation by [President Barack] Obama that left religious employers with clean hands and turned the provision of the coverage over to the insurance companies did not, however, end the effort to get contraceptive coverage out of the Affordable Care Act. Nonetheless, state legislatures and the most extreme members of the Senate have introduced legislation that would effectively overturn the mandate and grant wide latitude to both religious and secular employers to refuse to provide coverage for contraception. Arizona is considering a bill that would not only require female employees to assure the employer they want birth control for other than contraceptive reasons but would also permit the employer to fire them.

In May 2012 Arizona governor Jan Brewer signed into law a bill that allows employers to deny health insurance coverage of birth control and also restricts women from accessing birth control for non-medical reasons. © Ron Sachs/Bloomberg via Getty Images.

The commonplace belief that the debate over contraception was settled is now unsettled. Perhaps that's because the settlement is both socially and legally more recent and less assured than we think, especially for the rapidly growing number of singles.

The Supreme Court's Stance on Contraception Access

Griswold only granted the right to use contraception to married couples. Unmarried sexually active women (and men) gained the same right only on March 22, 1972, when the United States Supreme Court decided that unmarried couples had the same right as married couples to possess contraceptives.

The case was *Eisenstadt v. Baird*, which, as the historian David Garrow has pointed out, is "relatively unheralded" as a link between *Griswold* and *Roe v Wade*. *Eisenstadt* was a Massachusetts case (yes, the one state that gave its electoral votes to George McGovern later that year), triggered by activist Bill Baird's act of civil disobedience, providing contraceptive foam to a woman at Boston University. It was only one of a number of arrests Baird had invited during his multi-year crusade on behalf of legalization of access to contraceptives. While working for a medical supply company, on a visit to a hospital where he was demonstrating equipment, he had seen a woman die with a piece of coat hanger stuck in her cervix.

Had *Eisenstadt* not been so quickly followed by *Roe v Wade*, surely those morally opposed to unmarried sex would have been more engaged in public efforts to overturn that decision, but their horror over the affirmation of a right to choose abortion took precedence.

And *Eisenstadt* was left alone. But it is *Eisenstadt*—which created the right of unmarried people to use contraception—that social conservatives are now attacking. It is sexual activity by certain groups that is unacceptable. In the early twentieth century, those with poor genetic prospects were the ones whose sexual activity and reproduction was unacceptable. The eugenics movement dominated. Before World War II, many opposed contraception both because it violated "natural law" but also, openly, because it would likely mean a decline of the relative numbers of white people. C.S. Lewis, an iconic figure among conservative Christian intellectuals, whose *Chronicles of Narnia* have charmed so many children, was at best poorly disposed to contraception because, he reasoned, it represented the tyranny of the living over those not yet alive, as well as the prospect of promiscuity. But another skeptic of "family planning" was that exemplary anti-fascist George Orwell, apparently out of fear about the decline of manliness following the catastrophic losses of the best male British stock in the Great War. Eugenic arguments are now focused on race rather than mental disabilities. Single black women are especially targeted.

The Current Opposition to Contraception

But in the current round of opposition to contraception, all sexually active single women—and especially and paradoxically single women who have children—are suspect. When [CNN Republican presidential candidate debate host] John King asked [2012 Republican presidential candidate] Rick Santorum why he thought contraception was "dangerous," Santorum talked at length about the "problem in our culture with respect to children being raised by children, children being raised out of wedlock, and the impact on society economically, the impact on society with respect to drug use and all—a host of other things when children have children." Santorum's overwrought moralism betrayed his confusion: these problems follow from the *lack* of access to contraception by the young and poor, not access to it.

For his part, [2012 Republican presidential candidate Mitt] Romney wants to get rid of Planned Parenthood, which of course is where poor women and teens obtain contraception. We can hear an echo of the eugenics movement in Santorum's rant: instead of embracing contraception as a way to keep "undesirables" from having children, social conservatives want them to stop having sex.

Limbaugh, on the other hand, represents the ongoing fear of liberated women, uncontrolled by the civilizing aspect of

SUPPORT FOR CONTRACEPTION COVERAGE REQUIREMENT

Percent that support the US federal requirement that private health insurance plans cover the cost of birth control

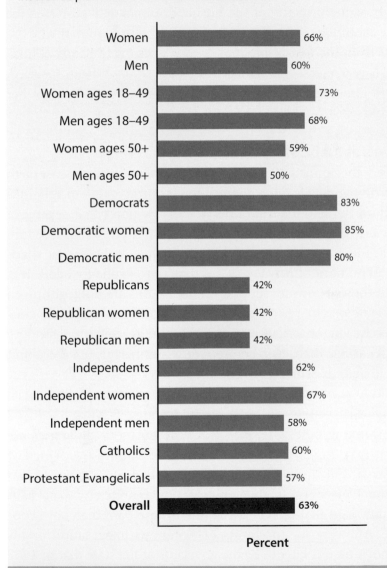

	Percent
Women	66%
Men	60%
Women ages 18–49	73%
Men ages 18–49	68%
Women ages 50+	59%
Men ages 50+	50%
Democrats	83%
Democratic women	85%
Democratic men	80%
Republicans	42%
Republican women	42%
Republican men	42%
Independents	62%
Independent women	67%
Independent men	58%
Catholics	60%
Protestant Evangelicals	57%
Overall	63%

Taken from: Kaiser Family Foundation, Health Tracking Poll, conducted February 13–19, 2012.

marriage and husband. In *Liberty and Sexuality*, Garrow quotes extensively from conservative commentators who claim that *Eisenstadt* was intended to legitimize sexual liberty and to extend separate the privacy right from marriage and family. Privacy, up to then, was essentially a patriarchal concept with the family as the property of the husband. Limbaugh expresses the same sentiment in cruder ways. Sexually active women who are freed from the fear of pregnancy are "sluts." Had Sandra Fluke, the 30-year-old single Georgetown Law student, been married, would Limbaugh have ranted that she wanted us to "pay for her to have sex?" We doubt it.

A Debate About Sexual Liberty

Indeed, the opposition to the Affordable Care Act's no-cost birth control mandate is not actually about contraception or religious freedom but about sexual liberty. Garrow notes that several of the clerks for the *Eisenstadt* justices suspected sexual freedom was as much a part of the thinking of the justices as was the shadowy penumbra of privacy rights that were explicitly cited. It is about those whose consensual sexual unions are not legitimized by a state or sanctified by a faith. Today more women are simply eschewing marriage or postponing it, as well as postponing childbearing, than ever before, yet a simmering unease about unmarried sex remains.

Only forty years have passed since *Eisenstadt*. No social change that young can but have its frailties. If we are seduced into thinking otherwise, it is partly because our memories are short. Take, for example, that young man who was studying law at Harvard at the time of *Eisenstadt*, just down the road from Boston University. In the January 12 Republican debate Mitt Romney said that he "can't imagine a state banning contraception." Allowing for the limits of Romney's imagination or his memory, he was later to be the governor of the state that in 1967 invoked its own prohibition of contraception for unmarried people and sent Bill Baird to prison.

Presumably, Romney was expressing the view that that was then and this is now. But can we be so sure? Will Rogers said, "The short memories of American voters is what keeps our politicians in office." Or perhaps puts them there.

| *"The birth-control mandate violates both statutory law and the Constitution."*

Birth-Control Mandate: Unconstitutional and Illegal

David B. Rivkin Jr. and Edward Whelan

In the following viewpoint, David B. Rivkin Jr. and Edward Whelan argue that the birth-control coverage mandate within the 2010 Patient Protection and Affordable Care Act, or ObamaCare, is a violation of religious freedom guaranteed by the First Amendment to the US Constitution. The authors claim that it also violates the Religious Freedom Restoration Act by failing to be the least restrictive way to achieve birth-control access and by lacking justification in the form of a compelling government interest. Rivkin represented twenty-six states in their challenge to ObamaCare and served in the US Department of Justice under Presidents Ronald Reagan and George H.W. Bush. Whelan is president of the Ethics and Public Policy Center and served in the US Department of Justice under President George W. Bush.

Last Friday [February 10, 2012], the White House announced that it would revise the controversial ObamaCare birth-

Protestors rally against the birth-control coverage mandate within the Affordable Care Act. Opponents of the mandate believe it is a violation of religious freedom to require employers to provide health insurance coverage for birth control. © Timothy A. Clary/AFP/Getty Images.

control mandate to address religious-liberty concerns. Its proposed modifications are a farce.

The Department of Health and Human Services would still require employers with religious objections to select an insurance company to provide contraceptives and drugs that induce abortions to its employees. The employers would pay for the drugs through higher premiums. For those employers that self-insure, like the Archdiocese of Washington, the farce is even more blatant.

The birth-control coverage mandate violates the First Amendment's bar against the "free exercise" of religion. But it also violates the Religious Freedom Restoration Act. That statute, passed unanimously by the House of Representatives and by a 97-3 vote in the Senate, was signed into law by President Bill Clinton in 1993. It was enacted in response to a 1990 Supreme Court opinion, *Employment Division v. Smith.*

That case limited the protections available under the First Amendment's guarantee of free exercise of religion to those government actions that explicitly targeted religious practices, by subjecting them to difficult-to-satisfy strict judicial scrutiny. Other governmental actions, even if burdening religious activities, were held subject to a more deferential test.

The 1993 law restored the same protections of religious freedom that had been understood to exist pre-*Smith*. The Religious Freedom Restoration Act states that the federal government may "substantially burden" a person's "exercise of religion" only if it demonstrates that application of the burden to the person "is in furtherance of a compelling governmental interest" and "is the least restrictive means of furthering" that interest.

The law also provides that any later statutory override of its protections must be explicit. But there is nothing in the ObamaCare legislation that explicitly or even implicitly overrides the Religious Freedom Restoration Act. The birth-control mandate proposed by Health and Human Services is thus illegal.

The refusal, for religious reasons, to provide birth-control coverage is clearly an exercise of religious freedom under the Constitution. The "exercise of religion" extends to performing, or refusing to perform, actions on religious grounds—and it is definitely not confined to religious institutions or acts of worship. Leading Supreme Court cases in this area, for example, involve a worker who refused to work on the Sabbath (*Sherbert v. Verner*, 1963) and parents who refused to send their teenage children to a public high school (*Wisconsin v. Yoder*, 1972).

In the high-school case, the Supreme Court found that even a $5 fine on the parents substantially burdened the free exercise of their religion. Under the Patient Protection and Affordable Care Act, employers who fail to comply with the birth-control mandate will incur an annual penalty of roughly $2,000 per employee. So it is clearly a substantial burden.

Objecting employers could, of course, avoid the fine by choosing to go out of business. But as the Supreme Court noted in *Sherbert v. Verner*, "governmental imposition of such a choice

Government Interference with Religious Freedom

There are places where even sincere religious faith must give way. Do you believe that a god commands child sacrifice? Too bad. You can't violate the rights of others in the name of religion.

In most cases, however, it is the government that should back off. Demanding that people violate their most sacred commitments ensures social conflict. Unless the interest is genuinely important, it makes little sense for the government to impose its will. Ordering every American to subsidize contraception does not qualify. In this case the simple state of liberty benefits everyone. You want it, you pay for it. You don't want it, you don't pay for it.

But now the government says no to choice. It doesn't matter what you want.

Doug Bandow, "Mandating Contraception,"
American Spectator, March 1, 2012.
www.spectator.org.

puts the same kind of burden upon the free exercise of religion as would a fine imposed against" noncompliant parties.

The birth-control mandate also fails the Religious Freedom Restoration Act's "compelling governmental interest" and "least restrictive means" tests.

Does the mandate further the governmental interest in increasing cost-free access to contraceptives by means that are least restrictive of the employer's religious freedom? Plainly, the answer is no. There are plenty of other ways to increase access to contraceptives that intrude far less on the free exercise of religion.

Health and Human Services itself touts community health centers, public clinics and hospitals as some of the available alternatives; doctors and pharmacies are others. Many of the entities, with Planned Parenthood being the most prominent, already furnish free contraceptives. The government could have the rest of these providers make contraceptive services available free and then compensate them directly. A mandate on employers who object for religious reasons is among the most restrictive means the government could have chosen to increase access.

The mandate also fails the "compelling government interest" test. Given the widespread availability of contraceptive services, and the far less restrictive other ways to increase their availability, the government can hardly claim it has a "compelling" interest in marginally increasing access to birth control by requiring objecting employers to join in this effort.

The "compelling interest" claim is further undercut by the mandate's exclusion, for purely secular reasons, of employers who offer "grandfathered" plans. These are employer-provided plans that existed at the time ObamaCare was enacted and can continue to operate so long as they do not make major changes. They cover tens of millions of enrollees, according to a recent estimate by Health and Human Services.

In an effort to rally its base in the upcoming November [2012] election, the Obama administration seems more interested in punishing religiously based opposition to contraception and abortion than in marginally increasing access to contraception services. It is the combination of the political motive, together with the exclusion of so many employers from the mandate, that has profound constitutional implications. It transforms the mandate into a non-neutral and not generally applicable law that violates the First Amendment's Free Exercise Clause.

In short, the birth-control mandate violates both statutory law and the Constitution. The fact that the administration promulgated it so flippantly, without seriously engaging on these issues, underscores how little it cares about either.

> "Over the counter access to oral
> contraceptives would allow many more
> women to experience the liberation
> of safe, noninvasive, and . . . morally
> acceptable reproductive freedom."

The Birth Control Pill Should Be Available Over the Counter

Jessica Sheehy

*In the following viewpoint, Jessica Sheehy argues that oral con-
traceptives should be available without a prescription because the
pills are effective, safe, and widely used. Sheehy claims that requiring women to see a doctor for a prescription is overly cumbersome
and interferes with women's reproductive rights. She concedes that
there are legitimate risks for women taking the birth control pill,
but she claims this is true of all over-the-counter medications, and
package labels can address this concern. At the time this viewpoint
was written, Sheehy was an intern for the Communications and
Policy Department of the American Humanist Association.*

With the passing of the pill's fiftieth birthday, much ink has
been spilled over the effect oral contraception has had
since its initial release in 1960. Women's rights have certainly
progressed in leaps and bounds as women took control of their
reproductive systems and took advantage of the opportunities

Jessica Sheehy, "The Pill: Still Safe, Effective, and Threatening After All These Years,"
Humanist, vol. 70, no. 5, September–October 2010, pp. 4–5. Copyright © 2010 by Humanist.
All rights reserved. Reproduced by permission.

Laws allowing teens to access the morning-after pill without a prescription have spurred debate. Some argue that requiring a prescription violates teens' reproductive rights. © Elise Amendola/AP Images.

this allowed them, flooding universities and business. The pill's level of involvement in the women's movement depends on who you ask—some say it created the movement, others believe its effect is exaggerated due to coincidental timing. Its exceptional performance or efficacy, however, cannot be overstated.

Making Oral Contraceptives Available Over the Counter

Oral contraceptives are among the most widely prescribed, consistently used, safe, and effective drugs available. Approximately 12 million U.S. women and over 100 million women worldwide use them. The birth control pill is 99 percent effective when used as directed, which, when accounting for missed pills or irregular dosing, translates to about 95 percent in practice. And unlike other birth control methods, oral contraceptives have yet to lose popularity in lieu of an alternate method. Beyond safe prevention of pregnancy, the pill, when taken consistently over a long period of time, has been linked to a decreased risk of ovarian cancer. In addition, oral contraceptives regulate a woman's menstrual cycle and often give her lighter periods with alleviated pre-menstrual symptoms. They can even clear up skin for women who suffer from persistent acne.

After half a century of such success, there is the possibility of another revolutionary advancement in the pill's future: over-the-counter (OTC) availability.

With a world of options open to her, today's woman is often balancing an education or a career, perhaps a family and more, which means getting to the doctor for a prescription can be a hassle. Even worse, it can be an impossibility for women without health insurance and for teens who can't go through a family doctor or access a clinic. Providing an OTC oral contraceptive would increase access, lower the cost, and again change the way women view birth control.

While the idea has sparked controversy, the truth is that we're already part of the way there. Pharmacies in the United States distribute emergency contraception ("the morning-after pill") without a prescription and traditional oral contraceptives are available over the counter in numerous countries around the world. Recent studies conducted in the Southwest have found that an increasing number of U.S. women choose to buy their birth control pills in Mexico because it's easier to cross the border than go to the doctor for a prescription.

The pill even got some rare, albeit vague, support in May [2010] from the National Association of Evangelicals when they released a statement saying they wanted to partner with groups providing contraception in order to reduce the number of abortions. But a month later conservative groups, including the Heritage Foundation, the National Abstinence Education Association, and U.S. Conference of Catholic Bishops, voiced their opposition to the section of the new federal healthcare law that would require employers and insurance companies in all fifty states to fully cover the cost of prescription contraceptives (currently twenty-seven states do). "We don't want to see the sexual health of our young people compromised," said Valerie Huber, executive director of the abstinence education group. "We are concerned that if there isn't a policy correction, that will be the result." Deirdre McQuade of the Catholic bishops concluded: "Married women can practice periodic abstinence. Other women can abstain altogether. Not having sex doesn't make you sick." These recycled arguments continue to beg the question, who are we really trying to protect?

Restrictive Birth Control Policies Harm Women

A recent study conducted by the Guttmacher Institute determined that at least 40 percent of American girls are already on the pill, which is actually fewer than in most developed nations, and that the figure should, if anything, be higher. Approximately 757,000 teenage girls became pregnant in this country in 2006 alone, and 316,000 of those pregnancies resulted in abortions or miscarriages. Restrictive birth control policies don't shield teens from sex and they don't protect young bodies from the trauma of pregnancy or abortion. They simply make it more difficult for healthy, responsible youth to take precautions.

One argument against OTC oral contraceptives notes that most doctors require a woman to come in for a yearly gynecological examination in order to renew her birth control prescription. While the intention is benevolent—symptoms of cervical cancer often go undiagnosed without an exam—this forces women who don't immediately have the time or money for an exam to put themselves at further risk by going without birth control until they can see a gynecologist. It also makes women who don't wish to be examined, which is perfectly within their rights, feel bullied or violated by their doctor.

One could argue all day about the validity of the demand for an OTC oral contraceptive but when it comes down to it,

NONCONTRACEPTIVE BENEFITS OF BIRTH CONTROL PILLS

Many women use oral contraceptive pills for noncontraceptive reasons, including women who have never had sex.

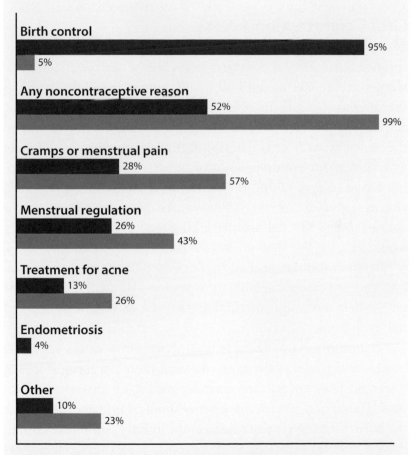

■ *Had sex in last 90 days*
■ *Never had sex*

Birth control
95%
5%

Any noncontraceptive reason
52%
99%

Cramps or menstrual pain
28%
57%

Menstrual regulation
26%
43%

Treatment for acne
13%
26%

Endometriosis
4%

Other
10%
23%

Among pill users, percent indicating reason

Taken from: Guttmacher Institute, "Contraceptive Use in the United States," July 2012. www.guttmacher.org.

this is a drug—not a lifestyle—that's been approved and it needs to be treated as such. This shouldn't be an issue of religion and morals but one of safety and legality. Like it or not, this is a secular state in which citizens—not the government—choose to live their lives according to their own beliefs. A woman's reproductive rights include the right to have sex without reproducing, and with the existence of safe options she shouldn't have to abstain from sex or be forced into a medical exam to exercise that right.

Oral Contraception Access Should Be Expanded

As wonderful as oral contraceptives can be for the majority of women, there are, as with all drugs, some legitimate concerns for outlying groups, and many challengers worry that if the drug can be bought over the counter it'll be flying off the shelves in the hands of every unsuspecting victim. Women over thirty-five who smoke, for example, do have an increased risk for developing blood clots if taking the pill (2 in 10,000 will experience a clot as opposed to 1 in 10,000 women who don't use the pill) and are often advised against taking oral contraceptives. They would not be the first group advised against taking an OTC medication, though, and all that's needed are some simple precautions and freely available information. All medications come with labels outlining instructions as well as warnings and red flag symptoms.

The unfortunate reality is that prescription drugs are being bought and sold illegally every day and there's nothing stopping a woman from giving her monthly packet of pills to an uninsured friend or timid niece who might not be informed about the risks. Furthermore, people who want to have sex rarely abstain just because they can't get oral contraceptives; they do it anyway and at a higher risk. With OTC availability, the issues surrounding birth control would be addressed more completely so that every woman could get the pill for herself and speak with a pharmacist if she so chooses.

To borrow [feminist] Carol Hanisch's well-worn phrase, the personal truly is political and women's opportunities can only extend as far as current policy allows. Over the counter access to oral contraceptives would allow many more women to experience the liberation of safe, noninvasive, and—for the overwhelming majority—morally acceptable reproductive freedom. Fifty years after the pill's birth, perhaps it's time we give it to them.

Organizations to Contact

The editors have compiled the following list of organizations concerned with the issues debated in this book. The descriptions are derived from materials provided by the organizations. All have publications or information available for interested readers. The list was compiled on the date of publication of the present volume; the information provided here may change. Be aware that many organizations take several weeks or longer to respond to inquiries, so allow as much time as possible.

Advocates for Youth
2000 M Street NW, Suite 750
Washington, DC 20036
(202) 419-3420 • fax: (202) 419-1448
website: www.advocatesforyouth.org

Advocates for Youth is an organization that works both in the United States and in developing countries with a sole focus on adolescent reproductive and sexual health. Advocates for Youth champions efforts that help young people make informed and responsible decisions about their reproductive and sexual health through its core values of rights, respect, and responsibility. Advocates for Youth publishes numerous informational essays available on its website, including "Emergency Contraception: A Safe and Effective Contraceptive Option for Teens."

American Center for Law and Justice (ACLJ)
PO Box 90555
Washington, DC 20090-0555
(800) 296-4529
website: www.aclj.org

The American Center for Law and Justice is dedicated to protecting religious and constitutional freedoms. ACLJ has participated in numerous cases before the US Supreme Court, Federal Court of Appeals, Federal District Courts, and various state courts regarding freedom of religion and freedom of speech. ACLJ has numerous memos and position papers available on its website and radio recordings, including "Birth Control and Minors."

American Civil Liberties Union (ACLU)

125 Broad Street, 18th Floor
New York, NY 10004
(212) 549-2500
email: infoaclu@aclu.org
website: www.aclu.org

The American Civil Liberties Union is a national organization that works to defend Americans' civil rights as guaranteed in the US Constitution. The ACLU works in courts, legislatures, and communities to defend First Amendment rights, the right to equal protection, the right to due process, and the right to privacy. The ACLU publishes the semiannual newsletter *Civil Liberties Alert* as well as briefing papers, including "Birth Control: A Game Changer for Women."

Center for Reproductive Rights

120 Wall Street
New York, NY 10005
(917) 637-3600 • fax: (917) 637-3666
email: info@reprorights.org
website: www.reproductiverights.org

The Center for Reproductive Rights is a global legal advocacy organization dedicated to reproductive rights. The Center for Reproductive Rights uses the law to advance reproductive freedom as a fundamental human right that all governments are legally obligated to protect, respect, and fulfill. The Center for

Reproductive Rights publishes articles, reports, and briefing papers, among which is the article "The Contraception Controversy: A Comprehensive Reply."

Concerned Women for America (CWA)

1015 Fifteenth Street NW, Suite 1100
Washington, DC 20005
(202) 488-7000 • fax: (202) 488-0806
website: www.cwfa.org

Concerned Women for America is a public policy women's organization that has the goal of bringing biblical principles into all levels of public policy. CWA promotes biblical values on six core issues—family, sanctity of human life, education, pornography, religious liberty, and national sovereignty—through prayer, education, and social influence. Among the organization's brochures, fact sheets, and articles available on its website is "Abortion Drugs Compliments of Neighbors and Friends."

Guttmacher Institute

125 Maiden Lane, 7th Floor
New York, NY 10038
(212) 248-1111 • fax: (212) 248-1951
website: www.guttmacher.org

The Guttmacher Institute works to advance sexual and reproductive health worldwide through an interrelated program of social science research, public education, and policy analysis. The Guttmacher Institute collects and analyzes scientific evidence to make a difference in policies, programs, and medical practice. The institute's monthly *State Policies in Brief* provides information on legislative and judicial actions affecting reproductive health, such as the recent brief "An Overview of Minors' Consent Laws."

Human Life Foundation, Inc.

353 Lexington Avenue, Suite 802
New York, NY 10016
website: www.humanlifereview.com

The Human Life Foundation, Inc. is a nonprofit corporation with the goal of promoting alternatives to abortion. The organization works toward this goal through educational and charitable means. The foundation publishes *The Human Life Review*, a quarterly journal that focuses on abortion and other life issues.

NARAL Pro-Choice America

1156 15th Street NW, Suite 700
Washington, DC 20005
(202) 973-3000 • fax: (202) 973-3096
website: www.naral.org

NARAL Pro-Choice America advocates for privacy and a woman's right to choose. NARAL Pro-Choice America works to elect pro-choice candidates, lobbies US Congress to protect reproductive rights, and monitors state and federal activity in the courts related to reproductive rights. The organization publishes numerous fact sheets, including "The Difference Between Emergency Contraception and Early Abortion Options."

National Right to Life Committee (NRLC)

512 10th Street NW
Washington, DC 20004
(202) 626-8800
email: nrlc@nrlc.org
website: www.nrlc.org

The National Right to Life Committee was established to repeal the right to abortion after the decision in *Roe v. Wade* (1973). The NRLC works toward legislative reform at the national level to restrict abortion. NRLC publishes a monthly newspaper, the *National Right to Life News,* and several fact sheets, such as "Guarantee Women's Access to Birth Control."

National Youth Rights Association (NYRA)

1101 15th Street NW, Suite 200
Washington, DC 20005
(202) 835-1739
website: www.youthrights.org

The National Youth Rights Association is a youth-led national nonprofit organization dedicated to fighting for the civil rights and liberties of young people. The NYRA seeks to lower the voting age, lower the drinking age, repeal curfew laws, and protect student rights. NYRA's research collection, available at its website, has papers, studies, videos, and audio clips.

Planned Parenthood Federation of America

434 West 33rd Street
New York, NY 10001
(212) 541-7800 • fax: (212) 245-1845
website: www.plannedparenthood.org

Planned Parenthood is a sexual and reproductive health-care provider and advocate. Planned Parenthood works to improve women's health and safety, prevent unintended pregnancies, and advance the right and ability of individuals and families to make informed and responsible choices. On its website, Planned Parenthood offers information about birth control.

For Further Reading

Books

Peter C. Engelman, *A History of the Birth Control Movement in America*. Santa Barbara, CA: Praeger, 2011.

Angel M. Foster and Lisa L. Wynn, eds., *Emergency Contraception: The Story of a Global Reproductive Health Technology*. New York: Palgrave Macmillan, 2012.

Melissa Haussman, *Reproductive Rights and the State: Getting the Birth Control, RU-486, and Morning-After Pills and the Gardasil Vaccine to the US Market*. Santa Barbara, CA: Praeger, 2013.

David L. Hudson, *The Right to Privacy*. New York: Chelsea House, 2010.

N.E.H. Hull and Peter Charles Hoffer, *Roe v. Wade: The Abortion Rights Controversy in American History*. Lawrence, KS: University Press of Kansas, 2010.

Christopher Kaczor, *The Ethics of Abortion: Women's Rights, Human Life, and the Question of Justice*. New York: Routledge, 2011.

Catriona Macleod, *Adolescence, Pregnancy, and Abortion: Constructing a Threat of Degeneration*. New York: Routledge, 2010.

Elaine Tyler May, *America and the Pill: A History of Promise, Peril, and Liberation*. New York: Basic Books, 2010.

Heather Munro Prescott, *The Morning After: A History of Emergency Contraception in the United States*. New Brunswick, NJ: Rutgers University Press, 2011.

Rickie Solinger, *Reproductive Politics: What Everyone Needs to Know*. New York: Oxford University Press, 2013.

Bonnie Steinbock, *Life Before Birth: The Moral and Legal Status of Embryos and Fetuses.* New York: Oxford University Press, 2011.

Jessica Valenti, *The Purity Myth: How America's Obsession with Virginity Is Hurting Young Women.* Berkeley, CA: Seal Press, 2009.

Periodicals and Internet Sources

Daniel Allott, "Does *Roe* Still Matter?," *American Spectator*, January 25, 2012. www.spectator.org.

Caitlin Borgmann, "Abortion Parental Notice Laws: Irrational, Unnecessary and Downright Dangerous," *Jurist*, July 27, 2009. jurist.law.pitt.edu.

Rob Boston, "Barrier Methods: The Church's Ceaseless Opposition to Birth Control," *Humanist*, May/June 2012.

Rob Boston, "Contraceptive Controversy: Catholic Bishops, Religious Right Allies Step Up Their Campaign to Deny Americans' Access to Birth Control," *Church & State*, May 2012.

Irin Carmon, "Birth Control Doesn't Matter," *Salon*, May 11, 2012. www.salon.com.

Erika Christakis, "The Argument You *Don't* Hear About Birth Control in Schools," *Time*, September 26, 2012. www.time .com.

Tracy Clark-Flory, "Abstinence Isn't Working," *Salon*, April 15, 2012.

Chuck Donovan, "Encouraging the Abstinent Majority," *Pioneer Press*, July 4, 2010.

Family Planning and Contraceptive Research, "A Shifting Landscape: Parental Involvement Laws and Their Effect on Minors," University of Chicago Medical Center, January 13, 2010. www.chicagofamilyplanning.org.

Guttmacher Institute, "Facts on American Teens' Sexual and Reproductive Health," February 2012.

Christine Kim and Robert Rector, "Evidence on the Effectiveness of Abstinence Education: An Update," *Backgrounder*, no. 2372, February 19, 2010. www.heritage.org.

Amanda Marcotte, "Conservative Groups Demand High Abortion, Teen Pregnancy Rates," *Slate*, July 13, 2010. www.slate.com.

Jeanne Monahan and Robert Schwarzwalder, "Congress Should Make Secret Abortions Illegal," *National Review Online*, April 12, 2012. www.nationalreview.com.

Michael New, "Abortion Laws and Their Effects on Abortion Rates," *One Pager*, Family Research Council, July 2010. www.frc.org.

Nancy Northup, "Estranged Bedfellows: Sexual Rights and Reproductive Rights in US Constitutional Law," *Human Rights*, Spring 2011.

Joseph J. Sabia and Daniel I. Rees, "The Effect of Parental Involvement Laws on Youth Suicide," *Economic Inquiry*, January 2013.

Jennifer Senior, "The Abortion Distortion: Just How Pro-Choice Is America, Really?," *New York*, December 7, 2009.

Wesley J. Smith, "Abortion Now More Important than Parental Rights," *First Things*, March 24, 2010. www.firstthings.com.

Wesley J. Smith, "What About Religious Freedom? The Other Consequences of Obamacare," *Weekly Standard*, vol. 18, no. 7, October 29, 2012.

Margaret Talbot, "Taking Control," *New Yorker*, March 19, 2012.

Stuart Taylor Jr., "More Health Care Supreme Court Drama: 'Contraceptive Mandate' Versus Religious Freedom,"

National Journal, December 12, 2012. www.nationaljournal
.com.

Michael Tennant, "Teenage Girls Secretly Given Contraceptive
Implants and Injections in UK Schools," *New American*,
November 6, 2012.

Index